COTTAGE COUNTRY GHOSTS

Ontario Hauntings

Maria Da Silva
and Andrew Hind

GHOST
HOUSE

Ghost House Books

The Distributor: Lone Pine Publishing
10145 – 81 Avenue
Edmonton, AB T6E 1W9
Canada

Websites: www.ghostbooks.net
www.lonepinepublishing.com

Library and Archives Canada Cataloguing in Publication

Da Silva, Maria
       Cottage country ghosts / Maria Da Silva and Andrew Hind.

ISBN 978-1-894877-63-3

       1. Haunted places--Ontario. 2. Ghosts--Ontario. I. Hind, Andrew
II. Title.

BF1472.C3D38 2010   133.109713   C2010-903869-X

Editorial Director: Nancy Foulds
Project Editor: Sheila Quinlan
Production Manager: Gene Longson
Layout and Production: Janina Kuerschner
Cover Design: Gerry Dotto
Cover Image: iStock Photo (Trees and mist—John McLaird; Water in foreground—vesilvio)
Photo Credits: All photos are by Maria Da Silva and Andrew Hind except: p. 13 courtesy of Inn at the Falls; pp. 48, 151 courtesy of the Parry Sound Public Library; p. 61 courtesy of Yesterday's Resort; p. 198 courtesy of the Haliburton Highland Museum.

We acknowledge the financial support of the Government of Canada through the Book Publishing Industry Development Program (BPIDP) for our publishing activities.

Canadian   Patrimoine
Heritage   canadien

PC: 5

Dedication

To all our Muskoka friends who showed us things
that would otherwise be unseen.

Foreword

All of the stories presented within this book were extensively researched using archival material, newspapers, interviews with knowledgeable and relevant individuals and eyewitness accounts. The stories are intended to be entertaining and engrossing, but the most strenuous efforts have been made for accuracy, both in historical detail and in the retelling of our sources' ghostly encounters.

We should take the time to define Cottage Country, or at least Cottage Country as defined by this book. Cottage Country can mean a great many things to a great many people. It could refer to the Kawarthas, Haliburton, the Bruce Peninsula or even Simcoe County's Georgian Bay shores. But for most people, Cottage Country refers to the Muskoka and Parry Sound districts, and the near north just beyond them. Rather than cast our net so broadly as to do no area justice, we elected to hone in on the region most often associated with Ontario's Cottage Country.

Still, *Cottage Country Ghosts* is not a comprehensive book of hauntings from this vast and diverse region. To chronicle every supernatural story we came upon during the course of our research would have required a volume many times this size, and almost certainly even then there would be many stories omitted simply because we were unaware of them. Instead, this book contains our favourites, a representative sampling of the most flavourful tales from across the region. We are always looking for further stories to add to our files, and we welcome correspondence from readers. We can be reached via email at maelstrom@sympatico.ca or at dasilvababy@hotmail.com.

Many of the locations in this book are open to the public. Some are not. In all cases, please respect private property and people's personal beliefs. It reflects badly on all who have a passion for exploring our haunted history when such basic courtesies are not honoured.

Contents

Introduction

The landscape changes drastically as you cross the Severn River. The rolling farmland and lightly wooded countryside of Southern Ontario gives way to the dense forests, countless lakes and rivers and ever-present rock of Cottage Country— a hard landscape, but unmistakably beautiful at the same time. The transition is rapid, occurring in the blink of an eye, and you instantly know you're in a different world.

It's hard to imagine what the pioneers who settled this region must have felt when they encountered this harsh terrain for the first time, so different from anything they had seen in their homelands. They must have been intimidated by the towering trees, the wild animals that lurked in the shadows and the sheer isolation.

And yet, incredible as it may seem, they also initially viewed the land with optimism, and in their mind's eye they saw themselves transform the forests into bountiful fields of golden wheat. Back then, people believed that dense forests meant good soil for farming. By that naïve reasoning, Ontario's Cottage Country should be the richest of farmland because it is so thickly carpeted by trees that in some places the sunlight struggles to penetrate the foliage. But such beliefs were misplaced; the soil here is shallow and infertile, lying like a thin skin over the rocky skeleton of the landscape. It proved all but impossible to grow crops, and instead of bounty the settlers found only unrelenting heartache.

These settlers could not have survived without the logging industry, which moved into the region alongside them and began cutting down the forests to feed the insatiable demand for lumber in Toronto and the United States. Disheartened and weary from the backbreaking labour they'd put into unproductive farmland, farmers would have to leave their families and join logging camps for the winter simply to make ends meet. Doing so meant months of toil in the snow-covered woods, but without this income to supplement the meager gains from their bush lots, many families certainly would have starved.

Unfortunately, the lumbermen didn't put much thought into the sustainability of the region, and the long-term fortunes of the communities that depended upon the logging industry were of no consequence. Most companies' sole concern was to make quick profits. They attacked the land so rapaciously that within only two generations they had logged themselves out of business and were forced to move their operations farther north in search of new forests to exploit. Without the second income generated from working in the logging camps to fall back on, few farmers could make ends meet. They had no choice but to abandon their homesteads, either moving out west for the rich farmlands of the prairies or migrating to the cities.

But the region refused to die despite the loss of the logging industry and the demise of so many farms. Although the transition was difficult, the region eventually reinvented itself as a summer playground where people could enjoy the countless lakes, breathe fresh air, listen to the silence of the forests and find solace in the hospitality of a resort or the comfort of one's own vacation home. Thus was born Cottage Country, one of Canada's most popular tourist destinations.

There is another side to this region, however, one rarely seen and which is at odds with its reputation as a place for carefree leisure amidst rustic beauty—an underlying darkness that few talk about and fewer still witness. Ghost stories haunt Cottage Country's dense forests, deep lakes and quaint communities. They creep from shadow to shadow, existing out of sight of the frivolity that marks this land of cottages and resorts. They lurk under stones just waiting to be turned over.

And that's what we did. We turned over the stones, peered into the shadows and asked questions that few tourists care to ask. We found that though the rocky landscape was poor for farming, it was fertile ground for ghost stories. Muskoka and Parry Sound districts, and the regions just north of them, are full of fascinating stories involving spectral vessels floating across the waves, enchanting resorts where undead guests refuse to check out, murderers so evil their souls were cast out by the soil in which their bodies were interred, and spirits whose lives were tragically cut short by the hard nature of life in this frontier region.

What makes Cottage Country different from the rest of Ontario? What makes it so unusually haunted? It's probably that the region elicits the strongest of emotions. On the one hand, it's breathtakingly beautiful, and countless people over the past century and a half have fallen under its spell. It's the kind of place you want to return to, year after year…perhaps even in death. On the other hand, for many settlers it was a place of sorrow, broken dreams and broken bodies, and unimaginable hardship. Souls, tortured by unfulfilled lives, linger on in search of the contentment that escaped them in life.

When we were asked to write a book on Cottage Country ghosts, we jumped at the chance. This region is the kind of place that embraces you with its beauty, people and history. We've spent considerable time here, exploring the history and attractions while writing and enjoying carefree days at our cottages. We've grown close to people here. In many ways, it's like a second home to us.

We also have come to appreciate the vast diversity of Cottage Country. There are rapidly growing communities and a bounty of world-class resorts with the most modern amenities, but at the same time, there are the dense forests and pristine lakes dotted with small rural villages: a rarely changing region that is widely hailed as among Ontario's most beautiful. These are the facets that most often come to mind, the parts that form the centrepiece of tourist marketing. But there is a far greater depth to the region, including a rich heritage of spooks and strange happenings that form a vital part of local folklore.

When the topic of Cottage Country's ghosts and ghouls comes up, the same three locations invariably become the focus of conversation: the Bala Bay Inn, the Gravenhurst Opera House and the Severn River Inn. But while these places are justifiably famous for their otherworldly inhabitants, there are many lesser known but no less intriguing haunts that exist within the shadowy nether regions of Cottage Country. In fact, it seems as if each village or town has a ghost story, and that every person you speak to will recall something that was just plain spooky.

To some people, ghost stories are in the same category as tabloids and are better found on the bottom shelf of a supermarket magazine rack than in a serious book. More than once our inquiries into local folklore were met with skepticism, if not outright disbelief. Thankfully, such responses were heavily outweighed by the people who encouraged our work, shared their own personal experiences with the paranormal or offered their assistance in researching historical information. They recognized the value of what we were trying to accomplish with this book.

Ghost stories—or at least, ghost stories with context—reveal a great deal about the history of a place and its people, going beyond tragedies leading to death to encompass how people lived. In fact, ghost stories are as much history as they are horror. They should not be locked up and forgotten like a dark secret, but rather they should be shared. And by sharing, we keep these stories and the people within them alive, for the telling breathes new life into them. Maybe that's all ghosts want: to be remembered, to remain alive, if only in our thoughts.

Ghosts of Inn at the Falls

There are some places so warm and inviting that you just can't see yourself leaving, in life or in death. Inn at the Falls, a quaint, century-old inn located in the heart of Bracebridge, is just such a place. Hidden beneath the Victorian charm and warm hospitality of this historical building lies a mysterious otherworld that few people see, a realm inhabited by several ghosts who refuse to "check out" even when their stay on this earth has long since ended. With all the beauty that surrounds the building, these spectral guests are content to remain and welcome the visitors who come from near and far to experience the inn's unique atmosphere.

The building today known as Inn at the Falls was built in 1876 by John Adair when Bracebridge was still a frontier town, growing rapidly but still rough around the edges. A year later, Adair sold it to William C. Mahaffy, a lawyer, land surveyor and, from 1888, Muskoka's first district judge. The estate extended along the river and included much of what is today the community's downtown core.

Shortly after Judge Mahaffy's untimely death in 1912, his family sold the luxurious manor. It served for a time as a youth centre and orphanage but then fell vacant and into disrepair. Local youths began to refer to the decaying mansion as a haunted house, and perhaps there was something to it. Spectral occupants may have made potential owners uncomfortable, chasing them from the building before they could make it their own. This theory would certainly explain the rapid decline of the grand home, a home that just a few short years earlier was the most impressive one in town and that by all rights should have been in great demand.

Thankfully, the sad structure was saved from further decay by Edward Kirk and his wife, who purchased it in the 1920s and began an extensive restoration. It was to be their dream home, a place to raise their children and grow old together, but instead it brought heartache. A pregnant Mrs. Kirk fell down the stairs, the accident claiming her life and that of her unborn child. Devastated and inconsolable, Edward moved on, fleeing the painful memories held within the building.

Once again, the former Mahaffy home was left vacant and awaiting rescue. In 1943, Ernie and Marion Allchin bought the property and transformed it into quaint bed and breakfast called Holiday House. It has been an inn ever since, but trouble still dogged it. In the early morning hours of October 20, 1955, a fire broke out on the top floor and rapidly began to spread down the hallways and through the rooms. Luckily, a guest noticed the smoke and sounded the alarm, allowing everyone to escape unharmed. Firemen rushed to the scene, but despite their efforts the flames engulfed the entire upper floor and consumed everything in their path. The building was razed, and the owners were devastated. The loss was estimated at $40,000.

Rebuilding began almost immediately, resulting in the quaint building enjoyed by so many guests each year. Thankfully, much of the character of the original building was maintained during the reconstruction. In 1975 the building was purchased by Jim and Jackie Nivens, and then it changed hands again in 1988 when Peter and Jan Rickard became the proud owners. A new name, Inn at the Falls, signalled the change in ownership. The Rickards began to expand the inn to encompass four other historic buildings on the street, including the century-old former Salvation Army Citadel.

Bracebridge's Inn at the Falls is one of the most haunted locations in Cottage Country.

The Rickards, and every owner since, have openly admitted the inn is haunted by multiple spirits. A cheerful hotel that is charming and elegant and full of character, it exudes a timeless serenity. It's easy to see why guests and ghosts alike find it hard to pull themselves away. In fact, Inn at the Falls is so wrapped in ghostly myths and rumours that it is said to be the most haunted building in all of Muskoka. Every autumn it plays host to a popular ghost-themed weekend that includes exclusive tours, discussions about the inn's remarkable history and tradition of hauntings, and an opportunity to interact with psychics.

At last count, there were at least five identifiable spirits here, clinging to the ancient bricks like mortar. We will explore three of the ethereal residents that guests frequently encounter: a female ghost that lurks within a shadow-filled room in the basement, a lost and confused Ojibwa maiden and Judge William C. Mahaffy himself.

Judge William C. Mahaffy

The guest registry at Inn at the Falls seems full of ghosts, but foremost of these otherworldy guests is former owner Judge William C. Mahaffy. He was one of the most powerful and influential men in 19th-century Muskoka, and it was in this grand old building that Mahaffy lived, raised his children, entertained friends and family, conducted business—and most likely left a little piece of himself behind. His commanding presence is most definitely still felt at Inn at the Falls to this day.

Born on March 1, 1849, William Cosby Mahaffy was the son of Doctor John Mahaffy, a well-respected Simcoe County physician. The elder Mahaffy was one of the leading citizens in the village of Bond Head (located south of Barrie), so from an early age William learned about public duty and responsibility. His father's example had a profound influence on his life.

Despite a rural upbringing, William Mahaffy received an excellent education that began in the local one-room schoolhouse and ended with a law degree from the University of Toronto. Upon graduation, the young lawyer accepted a position in a Barrie law firm. The next few years were undistinguished, though he must have done well enough to catch the eye of Sarah Jesse, the daughter of a prominent politician and a prize catch for an up-and-comer such as himself.

Once happily married, Mahaffy began to search for ways to advance his career. Serving as a junior lawyer in a firm was restrictive and meant his future was tied to the whims of his bosses, which didn't sit well with him. In 1877, Mahaffy and his new wife vacationed in Bracebridge, a community that was rapidly growing but remained poorly served by lawyers. That chance trip to Muskoka proved life changing. The ambitious attorney decided this frontier town represented a golden opportunity to escape the shadows of elder lawyers and to make his own mark. Bracebridge was the perfect place for social and career advancement, a place where he could become a leading figure if only he played his cards right. He decided move there, and that decision started his rapid rise.

Mahaffy opened his own law practice and purchased arguably the finest home in town, an elegant manor called The Rockies, perched atop a hill overlooking Bracebridge's thundering waterfall (a home that is today the centrepiece of Inn at the Falls). It wasn't long before he had earned for himself a glowing reputation both as a lawyer and a citizen, and it came as little surprise to anyone that he was named the first district judge for Muskoka and Parry Sound on June 14, 1888. William Mahaffy was only 39 years old, making him the youngest judge in all of Canada at the time.

In addition to serving as a judge, Mahaffy improved his finances through land speculation and real estate development. It wasn't long before he was one of the largest landholders in Bracebridge, owning significant portions of the community's core and along the banks of the Muskoka River. While he was growing wealthy, Mahaffy was also rising within the ranks of influential fraternities such as the Loyal Orange Lodge, the Imperial Federation League and the Ancient Order of United Workmen. In short, throughout the 1890s he cemented his hold on power in the region.

At the same time, Mahaffy's family was growing. His three sons, Darcy, George and Montague Mahaffy, were raised in wealth and privilege, growing into men within the walls of The Rockies. While none reached the heights of their father, all rose to some measure of prominence in Muskoka. Mahaffy had reason to be proud of his children.

Around 1910, Mahaffy's health suffered a precipitous decline, and by 1912 he was clearly dying. He ventured to England in search of treatment but never returned home, passing away on July 12, 1912, at the age of 63. All of Muskoka went into mourning upon hearing the news. Yet although Judge Mahaffy's body was buried in Britain, his spirit returned to the place he felt most at peace. With so many happy memories tied to his beloved home, is it any wonder that he refused to let go? Even when the building was subsequently made into an inn, he continued to preside over it, seemingly unaware that it was no longer his private sanctuary.

He remains there to this day, appearing before numerous startled witnesses and mischievously moving items around. Many times guests and staff have reported seeing a tall, older man, well-dressed in a long, black, tailed jacket, grey pinstriped pants and black shoes and with a handlebar moustache, walking imperiously around the inn. He seems completely at home, as if he has as much right—or perhaps more so—as the witnesses themselves to be in the building. Two rooms in particular seem to be favoured by Mahaffy's spirit: the parlour and the Fox and Hounds Pub.

The Fox and Hounds is located in the building's basement, in what was at one time a stable. The pub itself is warm and inviting, a perfect replica of that which might be found in small-town Britain. But to get to the pub, one walks through almost maze-like corridors and under stone archways that create an atmosphere that is at once undeniably charming and unaccountably chilling.

The pub is a hotspot of supernatural activity. Several people have seen Mahaffy's ghost here, an apparition with the steely gaze, ramrod-straight body and hard face of a man used to getting his way. A quick comparison with a portrait of the former owner that used to hang in the inn leaves no doubt about the ghost's identity. Even when Mahaffy is not seen he makes his presence felt, as countless people have witnessed inexplicable phenomena that have been attributed to his restless spirit. Glasses will rattle on their own without explanation, cold drafts suddenly appear and just as suddenly disappear, and ghostly orbs are captured on camera. A waitress was left quivering when, as if by invisible hand, ice rose up from behind the bar and was thrown about the room. Then there was the time when a staff member was about to flick the switch to turn off the lights for the night. Her hand froze when she heard a male voice say, "Don't turn off the lights." It was an order, not a request. The woman was alone and wasn't about to disobey a ghost, so she left the lights on and went home. Another waitress saw a distinguished-looking gentleman calmly sitting in a chair, watching her intently for a few moments, before suddenly vanishing before her eyes.

Once, in the late 1990s, a night-shift bartender noticed a gentleman walk past the bar and down the short hall to the bathroom. The man was oddly dressed in period attire, clothes better suited to the 1890s than the 1990s, which the bartender thought odd. But in truth, at the time he didn't think much about it. Instead he remembers being more than a little annoyed because it was only a few minutes to midnight and he desperately wanted to close up for the evening. His annoyance became more intense as long minutes passed and the gentleman did not return. Finally, motivated by a mixture of concern and anger, the bartender decided to check up on the man, but upon entering the bathroom he found it completely empty. He was puzzled. The only way out of the bathroom was back through the pub, in which case it would have been impossible for the bartender not to have noticed the man leave. It was as if the man had simply vanished into thin air. Perhaps he had.

More than one witness has reported seeing the judge in the pub walking several inches off the ground. This apparent elevation makes sense historically because stables would have had a sub-floor, six to eight inches above ground, to allow for better drainage. This sub-floor was removed during the renovations that saw the home transformed into an inn, so witnesses who claim to see the ghost floating are probably just seeing Mahaffy walk across the floors as he knew them.

Cathy Morrow is one staff member who can boast of a face to face encounter with the judge. It happened one cold November morning, shortly after she had arrived to open the pub in anticipation of breakfast service. Cathy left the room for a few minutes to attend to other matters. As she returned down the stone-walled corridor, she caught sight of a wispy figure standing in one of the alcoves. The figure was wearing grey pinstriped pants, a long, black tailcoat and black shoes and floated about six inches off the floor. The ghost's face was distinct, and Cathy clearly identified him as Judge Mahaffy.

The two stared at one another for a few seconds, and then the judge faded from view.

Why does Mahaffy visit the pub? Some people suggest it's because he had a passion for horses that carried over into the afterlife. Others believe that the judge held secretive meetings with his Masonic fellows within one of the chambers located off of the stables, and that he returns to the site of these gatherings for companionship or to revel in the power associated with them. Both explanations are possible.

The other room for numerous ghostly sightings, the parlour on the inn's main floor, is the most frequented room in the inn, a beautiful place that manages to be both formal and relaxing with its dark hardwood floors, cosy Victorian-inspired chairs and log-burning fireplace. Functions are held here on occasion, but most often you'll find guests huddled around the crackling flames, chatting quietly or engrossed in a newspaper. The room was used in much the same fashion a century ago. Mahaffy likely spent many evenings sitting around the large fireplace (original to the building, having survived the fire), enjoying the company of family and close friends, perhaps indulging in a book or savoring a cigar. Maybe that's why staff and guests oftentimes report smelling the sweet aroma of cigar smoke coming from this room, even though the inn has a no smoking policy and no offender can ever be found. Mahaffy casually ignores the policy. It's his home, after all, and no one is going to tell him he can't light up a cigar if it pleases him to do so.

"The spectral activity seems to pick up in October and November, when there are fewer guests," says Krista Havenaar, a level-headed, professional businesswoman who served as innkeeper during our first visit to Inn at the Falls in

2005. "I wasn't a believer when I started working here, but I am now."

One event in particular was responsible for her change of heart. It was a hectic day as Krista raced about, setting up the inn for a wedding reception. The elegant parlour is always a focal point for such events, so Krista paid special attention to it. She knew the room would soon be full of guests and decided to turn the temperature down to make it more comfortable. She then turned on some soft, welcoming music. When Krista returned a few minutes later to ensure that the room met her exacting standards, she found the air absolutely stifling. She put her hand on the radiator and found it was pumping out heat full blast. She also noticed that the music had been turned off.

Krista checked on the thermostat, which was located behind a door that had been propped open and blocked by a large couch. It was up to 100 degrees. Confused, she adjusted the thermostat, turned the music on again, and left. "I wasn't gone 10 minutes when it happened again," she says. "I thought someone was playing with me, so I fixed the temperature again and hid nearby. A few minutes later, sure enough the room was hot again and the thermostat was up to 100 degrees. No one had entered the room. It was creepy."

Krista's experience is validated not only by other eyewitness accounts but also by photographic evidence. A photo taken at night clearly depicts a ghostly figure peering through the parlour's window. Only the upper torso is visible, but it's definitely a gentleman wearing judge's robes and a large white collar. It seems the ever-elusive Judge Mahaffy was caught on film, and the front desk is happy to share the image with anyone who asks to see it.

Many guests see Mahaffy and don't even realize they've had a paranormal experience. A few years back, a woman was sitting in Victoria's Restaurant across the hall from the parlour, enjoying a pleasant meal without even the slightest notion that the building was haunted to colour her perceptions. She happened to look up and saw a gentleman dressed in 19th-century judge's clothes—dark robes, wig, pinstriped suit—standing in the parlour, silently watching guests eat. The woman smiled at him and went back to her meal.

"She later mentioned to the waitress how impressed she was that we went the extra mile to create a historic atmosphere by hiring a re-enactor to play the role of Judge Mahaffy," relates Krista with a laugh. "The waitress was confused, of course, because we'd done no such thing. When the waitress checked the parlour to see if someone was there, she found it empty. The man—the ghost—had disappeared."

Janet Marsden is Inn at the Falls' friendly front desk manager, and in 16 uneventful years working at the inn, not once had she encountered anything unusual, not even during her seven years working in the downstairs pub where so many people—guests and staff alike—have had eerie experiences. Part of her wanted to see something out of the ordinary, if for no other reason than so she no longer felt left out. Janet finally had the experience she was waiting for one chilly January day.

"I went into the lounge first thing in the morning, and as soon as I entered I smelled the overwhelming scent of cigar smoke. The inn is a non-smoking building, so that made no sense to me, but the smell was really distinct. Then I became really uncomfortable in the lounge, like something didn't want me there, and I had to leave. That sort of thing had never happened to me before in all my years here. I'm often in the building alone and I'm never scared, but I was that day. I wouldn't go back in that room. The day started weird and it continued, because while I was cleaning the rooms upstairs I found every bathroom door closed, which we don't do; we usually leave them open. I just felt strange all day long, and I can't explain it."

Staff and guests alike are fascinated by the building's ghostly heritage and flock here to be caught up in a shroud of mystery. Every October or November, Inn at the Falls hosts a popular "Spirits Come Alive" evening, with ghost tours, an elegant dinner and overnight accommodations as part of the package. It's an opportunity to fully experience the history and mystery of the building.

While ghostly experiences are hardly common occurrences at Inn at the Falls, the mere possibility that a guest *might* have a paranormal encounter only adds to the inn's already considerable charm. Judge William Mahaffy hasn't yet realized he's no longer the master of this domain and wanders the building as if it's his own. And in a sense perhaps it does still belong to him; staff and guests alike come and go over the years, but his spirit remains.

Girl in the Basement

Most of us can never really know or understand the impulses that would drive someone to brutally murder another human, but anger and jealousy brought on by passion are common triggers for violence. An unresolved crime, especially one driven by such powerful emotions, is often all it takes to bring murder victims back to relive again and again the terror of their death. Only after justice has been served and the truth of their demise is brought to light will these ghosts pass easily over to the other side. So it may very well be for one of the ghosts that inhabits the inn, a tragic figure whose story has literally been buried beneath the building and purposefully forgotten.

For all its splendour and charm, there is one room at Inn at the Falls that has given many who dare to enter genuine chills. The room in question happens to be in the depths of the basement, off from the English-style pub, behind the staff's lunchroom. It's a room most guests wouldn't see or be interested in: a small, dark, musty-smelling space that is home to hydro boxes and stored items that seemingly haven't been used in a long time. But it's also reputed to be home to something else, something far more sinister. The room is generally off-limits to the public but becomes accessible during annual ghost tours. It's at this time that the public gets to experience what the staff has long sensed in this room— dark and oddly eerie at even the best of times, the atmosphere in this room on occasion inexplicably transforms into one of gloomy darkness and frightful dread.

During a recent tour of the building, a young woman accompanied by a few friends found herself here, standing before this very room. While her friends cautiously hung back, unwilling to enter the claustrophobic confines of the room, the woman ventured alone into the darkness. "And yet, I got the feeling that I wasn't alone. Someone or something was there with me. It was a dark presence, and it made me uncomfortable," recalls the woman, who we'll call Cassandra. She entered slowly, nervously. "There was a stench of decay that was so real and so strong that I knew if I didn't leave soon I'd be sick. Suddenly, and to my horror, I felt an ice-cold, bony, skeletal hand touch my shoulder. Catching the scream within my throat so as not to scare the rest of the group, I quickly turned to leave. Clearly I was not wanted in there. The feeling of dread was something I had never felt before, and it took me a while to get over the unpleasant sensation."

When she was calm enough to speak about her experience later, Cassandra described the stench as how she imagined rotting flesh would smell. No other tour member detected anything other than a faint mustiness. Cassandra also got the impression that the skeletal hand was that of a woman, someone who was sad and trapped forever within the inn's basement, and that the oppressive room was like a cell, holding the spirit captive within its darkened confines. And yet, while the experience clearly frightened Cassandra, it was also exhilarating. "We, my friends and I, left Inn at the Falls the next morning, and did so with a sense of fulfillment. Not everyone gets the chance to experience what I did the night before," she explains. "Not just at having explored into the history of the ghostly residents of the charming resort, but also at having experienced some of the paranormal phenomena associated with it. I felt that I might have even subconsciously channelled some of the ghosts' energy…their sadness and pain."

Waitress Kathryn Lefebvre regularly gets bad vibes about the basement room. "It's creepy in there," she says. "I've had a couple of experiences where the hair stands on the back of your neck and you get the feeling you shouldn't be there."

While we were researching this book we attempted to get Kathryn to follow us in, but she adamantly refused. Clearly her fear was real, something that gnawed at her soul. We entered the room cautiously, not really knowing what to expect. It was claustrophobic, long and narrow, the shelves piled high with little-used supplies. We breathed musty air, but Maria also detected an unwholesome smell she couldn't identify. The light from the outer room doesn't penetrate all the way into this space, so dark shadows lurked menacingly— there was a distinctly oppressive feeling in the air, not quite fear inducing, but unsettling nonetheless. We could see why staff might be reluctant to go in there, especially if they had had previous experiences with the inn's spirits or been subjected to chilling tales by longer-serving employees.

No one can positively identify "the girl in the basement," as this female spirit has come to be known, but when Judge Mahaffy owned the home, many servants came and went. Psychics and others who have encountered her believe that the lingering entity was one of these forgotten residents, a young woman who, even while she lived, would have been virtually anonymous.

Most 19th-century servants were not from the immediate area. Employers feared the young girls would gossip about the family with friends, and being prominent and well-to-do, they feared having their home life scandalized. As a result, they brought in girls who had no ties to the community. Life away from home would have been difficult for these young girls: their employers would have been quite demanding of them, there were many strict rules to follow, and living conditions could be less than pleasant, despite the wealth of the families that hired them. Live-in servants as young as 12 or 13 slept in attics, in basements or in places under the stairs where they would be unseen and unheard by the family. These rooms often would be damp, cold and dimly lit.

A servant's earnings were as little as $20 a year, or the equivalent of about $160 today.

One of the most common and difficult obstacles for the girls to overcome was the loneliness and isolation they felt. They had no time off to socialize with other girls, they would not be allowed to talk to members of the household unless spoken to (even then it was simply to answer the question and then be gone), and possible suitors were definitely out of the question. But even if a girl was fortunate enough to have a suitor, in some cases they didn't feel worthy of affection due to abuse by the man of the house, abuse that generally remained undocumented and unpunished because of the status of the men in question. After all, who would believe a mere servant over a powerful and influential gentleman?

Time to themselves was unheard of for live-in servants, with their hectic days beginning at 6 AM and ending at 11 PM. In a household like that of Judge Mahaffy, where there was only one or perhaps two female servants at a time, the tasks to be completed were nearly endless: washing and ironing clothes, doing dishes, scrubbing floors on hands and knees, cooking meals, dusting, carrying water to prepare baths, carrying coal to the fireplaces and on cold nights making sure the fire remained roaring in the hearth. But the most important of all tasks was to tend to the children.

If any of these young girls were ever to defy their employer, they would be dealt with by extreme punishment. And Judge Mahaffy was one of the most powerful men in the community; for any young girl to have gone against his wishes, no matter the demand, would have been foolish on her part. It would have meant a penalty in pay, loss of privileges, perhaps even loss of job. As a result, these young and naïve girls did what it took to make a living and remained hopeful of eventually making a loving family of their own. Sadly, in some extreme and tragic cases, servants who defied particularly vengeful masters would simply "disappear," and who would question their whereabouts with families so far away and no friends in the community?

Is that the fate that befell the female spirit who lingers in the shadowy recesses of Inn at the Falls' basement? Dini Zuest Wilcox, a clairvoyant consultant who offers insight into all spiritual matters, certainly thinks so. Dini is unusually gifted, with years of experience communicating with the other side, and has even lent her assistance to the police once or twice. During a recent walk through the inn, Dini honed in on the tragic basement ghost and came away with a sense of a young girl's troubled life and violent demise. We listened intently as she shared her intuition.

"I sense a young girl, a teenaged girl employed in the home as a maid, who met foul play and is buried somewhere within these side walls," Dini said with obvious anguish, pointing to a stone wall in the basement. "This young girl was being taken advantage of by the man of this house, a powerful man who was used to getting his way. They argued, and when she pulled away from his iron grip she slipped and fell, cracking her head on the floor. She died in terrible pain. The man panicked. How could he explain her death to the community? Difficult questions might be asked. He decided it was easier to avoid the scandal by bricking her body into the wall and telling people she had simply left his employment."

Dini isn't the only one to connect with the lingering spirit of this forlorn woman. A gentleman staying at the inn a few years ago was touched by her presence, and in a very tangible way. The guest, Sam, had fallen asleep in his room in front of the glowing television, overcome by total physical and emotional exhaustion. The past few months had been particularly trying, with problems at work and at home, and the stress had eventually caught up to him. When he awoke with a start, he realized he had overslept and was now late in meeting his family in the Fox and Hound Pub for their pre-Christmas dinner reunion. He threw on the first clothes that fell out of his suitcase and raced downstairs.

The historic building was alive with festive flourishes. Halls were decked with greenery, the warm glow of flames danced in the fireplace, and big bows finished off bushy wreaths. Sam could feel the Christmas spirit overwhelming him and was looking forward to spending time with his loved ones. Then, without warning, the warmth of holiday cheer was replaced by an unnatural chill.

"As I was walking down the hall in the basement leading to the pub, I felt a rather chilling coldness down my left arm," Sam remembers. "It was an unusual coldness, not like any kind of breeze coming through an open doorway, for example. As I walked, the chill almost caressed my hand, like the tender touch of a woman." Despite his haste, Sam paused momentarily to consider the odd sensation. He could swear the chill ran along his hand like delicate fingers, soft and reassuring. But while the caress was gentle and affectionate, he could feel the cold biting into his flesh and watched as his fingertips began to turn blue before his eyes. After perhaps a few seconds of lingering in the hall, the cold became too uncomfortable and Sam continued on his way. "I was sure I could feel someone walking beside me as I walked down the hall, almost holding my hand, but the feeling disappeared when I entered the pub," he continued. "I've always wondered who that was, because I'm certain it was a ghostly encounter. There were no doors or windows open through which a breeze could come, and no draft in the basement. It had to be a ghost."

We'll never know if foul play ever truly occurred in this building, but for some guests who walk through the basement of Inn at the Falls, there is no doubt that they feel a young woman's pain and suffering. Was she murdered in cold blood or did she die during a violent quarrel? Either end would explain why people experience an oppressive aura in her presence. "I sense her sadness and pain are slowly disappearing now that her story is coming to light," says Dini Zuest Wilcox, "now that her story is beginning, instead of ending."

Ojibwa Woman

Her hair is long, dark and silky, her skin the lustrous gold of someone who has spent countless days under the sun's rays, and her eyes are like two black pearls that glitter in the light. She is, in a word, stunning. She stands at the doorway, barefooted and wearing a simple dress that hangs to her ankles, her innocent beauty somehow charming even the most negative of souls. Meaning no harm and making no attempt to communicate with the startled witness, she simply stares at the person within the room and then suddenly fades into the night. Time and time again, guests who stay in the Mews at Inn at the Falls encounter this beautiful but confused maiden. But who is this lovely woman, and what brings her into this modern building? It's a question that has perplexed several guests who anticipate a sound sleep in a cozy bed only to experience restlessness and late-night visitations.

Unlike the other five buildings that comprise Inn at the Falls, the Mews does not date back a century. Of more recent construction, it offers contemporary motel-style accommodations. But what it lacks in nostalgia is more than made up by the glorious view; each of the rooms has a large picture window and balcony overlooking the roaring falls and wide expanse of the Muskoka River far below. At first glance, there's nothing here to suggest a connection with First Nations. But what if we dig a little deeper?

Muskoka was originally Huron land, but this people made only occasional use of the area for hunting and fishing. By 1650, Iroquois from New York State had taken over, and this land became their territory. Fifty years later the Iroquois themselves would be pushed out by the Ojibwa (also known as the Chippewa, or in their own tongue, Anishnabe—The People), a native tribe from Northern Ontario, and Muskoka was still Ojibwa domain at the time when Europeans arrived in Ontario. Indeed, the name Muskoka probably comes from the great Ojibwa chief, Mesqua Ukie, who was greatly admired by both the British and his own people.

Canoeing along the Muskoka River and portaging around Bracebridge Falls was a centuries old tradition practiced by Muskoka's Ojibwa people. The Ojibwa were a nomadic people who moved about when the seasons changed, using the lakes and rivers as early highways for their birch bark canoes. In the spring, they would begin their journey north to their summer grounds in the bountiful forests of Muskoka, where they would hunt, trap, fish and pick berries. Then, with the earliest signs that frost and snow were around the corner, they would hastily return to a more southern encampment along the shores of Lake Simcoe to wait out the harshness of the winter months.

As late as 1850, the provincial government assured the native people that this land would always be theirs, and that the land between the Severn River and the French River would be set aside as a native reserve. But it was not to be, and by 1860 the government was parcelling out the land to settlers and awarding logging rights to lumber companies, disrupting the native way of life and depriving the Ojibwa of their seasonal hunting and fishing grounds.

Because of their nomadic lifestyle, the Ojibwa did not build permanent villages. They did, however, establish temporary seasonal camps that may have been returned to on a yearly basis, and archaeological digs reveal that at least one such camp existed along the shores of the Muskoka River at what is now Bracebridge. In fact, a historical plaque in Kelvin Grove Park opposite the inn indicates the existence of the encampment, pointing out that this was a natural place to pause before attempting to go upstream.

Of course, where people lived they also died, so surely there were Ojibwa who succumbed to illness, disease or old age here. When one of their own passed away the Ojibwa would bury that person in a burial mound, and instead of a headstone with the deceased's name inscribed upon it, the burial mound would have a wooden marker inscribed with his or her memory. In many cases, a "spirit house" would be erected over the mound. But because the Muskoka River floods each spring, and the flood waters would have reached much higher along the riverbanks in centuries past before dams were ever built to control the flow, such mounds would have been logically placed on the higher ground above the river, perhaps on the very ground where the Mews at Inn at the Falls stands today.

But whether she was buried somewhere nearby or is simply a wayward ghost who decided to linger, the spectral Ojibwa maiden has become a fixture within the Mews. The out-of-place woman has been seen and felt several times in recent years, and always it is her beauty and innocence that witnesses come away with. On occasion, her presence is accompanied by more startling paranormal phenomena, including unearthly sounds, roiling mist that suddenly materializes and dramatic drops in temperature. It's as if the building, perhaps even the very land itself, has become polluted by her restless soul.

Karen McMullin is a publicist for Dundurn Publishing, one of the largest publishers in Canada. She is a woman who has achieved success in her profession, and she is necessarily serious-minded, focused and rational—not the type of person to engage in flights of fancy, in other words. Yet she had no hesitation admitting she had personally encountered the inn's wraith-like native woman and enthusiastically shared the experience.

"I was staying in the Mews at Inn at the Falls in October, and I did not know at the time of the stories that the inn was haunted. I was up late watching television and went to bed around 1 AM. I woke up in the middle of the night with the distinct impression that I was being watched. It wasn't a creepy feeling, more of an annoyance, like 'stop watching me, I can't sleep.' I rolled over and went back to sleep. In the morning, I remembered the sensation and had an image in my head of a young woman sitting on the edge of the other side of the bed from where I was sleeping. She had dark, straight hair and I recall trying to determine what she was wearing—I tried to put her in Victorian garb but for some reason it didn't work. I had a calm sense about the image, nothing unnerving. The image was like a photograph, this young woman sitting on the bed with her hands in her lap."

A few months later when Karen had to return to the inn for yet another book fair, she called to make a reservation and was asked by the attending desk clerk if she would like to stay in the Mews once more. But, recalling her experience and the uncomfortable feeling she had of being watched as she slept, Karen told the woman that she would prefer to stay in a room that was not haunted. The desk clerk laughed and obediently assigned her a different room, but she was clearly intrigued and asked Karen what had happened during her last stay. Karen gladly shared her experience with her.

Several weeks later, when Karen arrived at Inn at the Falls for her stay, the same desk clerk greeted her. This time, the clerk had a story of her own to share. Karen was stunned to learn that the inn had more than one resident ghost, but in fact several. A psychic had come to Inn at the Falls to see if she could channel any spirits that may haunt the main building, but she left after one day instead of the two days that were planned. There was simply too much psychic energy for her to deal with; it literally overcame her senses, coming across as a chorus of voices from which it was impossible to distinguish just one. The psychic did indicate that it was safe to say the inn, and that though its surrounding buildings have a lot of activity, none of it is malicious.

Karen also learned from the clerk that a group of archaeological students were working downhill from the inn and across the river on a flat area where they had discovered traces of a native settlement (the clerk was referring to Kelvin Grove Park). Since it was mentioned that Ojibwa people would bury their dead on high ground, it seemed possible to both Karen and the clerk that the ghostly woman appearing in the Mews might have been a member of this tribe who had been buried on site.

"It seemed that my young lady was potentially native Canadian, which is why I didn't see her in Victorian dress, and with hair dark and straight it would fit her background," Karen says, referring to her ghostly visitor. She hastens to point out that she wasn't at all frightened by the experience, merely intrigued. "My father wrote a book on séances," she explains. "I've been around ghosts and spiritualism since I was a teenager, so this stuff doesn't faze me—perhaps it's why she came to visit. It was an interesting experience, and one that I remember to this day and enjoy sharing."

But Karen's was not the only experience in and around the Mews. A few years ago, a young couple very much in love found themselves in Muskoka, exploring Bracebridge hand-in-hand by day and spending peaceful nights at Inn at the Falls. Mike and Kate loved the tranquility of Cottage Country and were pleased to find that their accommodations were warm and relaxed, perfectly in keeping with the setting. One evening, they stood on the balcony of their Mews room admiring the beautiful grounds and the flow of the Muskoka River below. With the inn being such a romantic place, the couple seemed to have eyes only for each other and revelled in every moment spent together. Nevertheless, after a while on the balcony, and with the sun sinking low behind the trees, Kate decided she was a bit tired from the day's excitement and wanted to go inside and lie down. Her husband caressed her cheek as she turned to walk away. "I'll be in shortly," he said after her.

Mike continued to enjoy the beautiful surroundings until his gaze came across what seemed like a white cloud forming a few dozen metres down the hillside. This *thing*—he could only call it a thing, because it defied easy definition—grew rapidly and started to travel toward him, seeping up the hillside. Soon, it was below him and hitting the side of the Mews building like misty waves. *Kind of weird behaviour for fog*, the man thought as he watched with ever-growing curiosity.

The bone white mist began to roll up the walls and then flowed over the balcony, surrounding Mike, who found himself rooted to the spot and unable to move even as wisps began to coil around his limbs and envelop his body like a shroud. He immediately felt a drop in temperature, as if a cold, wet blanket was thrown over him. The now-frightened man was growing so cold that he could feel his body tingle with chills, and instantly he felt a despondent and uneasy feeling come over him. "I swore that I heard sad Indian chanting accompanied by the sound of drums beating. It was only for a few seconds, but it felt so real that it left me filled with a sense of sadness," recalled the young man. After a few tense moments in which Mike seemed mesmerized by the echo of the drums, the singing and chanting died away and the mist began to dissipate as if blown away by a gust of wind.

Snapped back to his senses, Mike retreated into the room, seeking the comfort of his wife's presence. But it did little good; the impact of what he had experienced remained with the man long after. "The sadness I felt lingered with me all night," he says. "Even after joining my wife I still couldn't sleep. Did I actually see anything? Did I see a ghost? No. But I sensed people all around, hidden by the thick fog." Mike tossed and turned all night long, restless and still on edge from his experience. Several times he awoke and thought he heard the keening sound of a native death song rising on the wind outside, barely distinguishable from the thunder of the falls far below. He was glad when the sun peeked above the horizon and signalled the arrival of morning.

Mike believes he came into contact with an echo of an Ojibwa burial ceremony that still repeats itself years after it was originally performed. It's the only explanation that seems to make sense to him. And it strikes him as being particularly sad, because it means the young maiden must also hear the mournful songs that were chanted by her heart-broken family at her funeral, a painful reminder of the loved ones she left behind.

Of course, her time to leave this earth and be reunited with them is long past. How long will she remain at Inn at the Falls, a lost soul, wandering aimlessly down hallways and appearing in rooms to sadly gaze upon guests? One can only hope that one day soon she will realize that she no longer belongs to this world and will cross over to be reunited with those who shed tears over her grave centuries ago.

The *Segwun* Ghost

The sun's hot rays shine down upon the crystal-clear waters, slowly lifting away the morning mist. It promises to be a beautiful summer day, and very soon tourists will begin arriving for yet another memorable cruise aboard Muskoka's most historic vessel, an elegant steamship that has withstood the test of time. It remains tied to the past even as the rest of Muskoka has marched onward into the 21st century.

This steamship, the RMS (Royal Mail Ship) *Segwun*, has seen many passengers and crewmen come and go during the years since its launch in 1887. The experience of sailing aboard her has changed little over the years, and it's a cruise you don't easily forget; with a loved one in tow, or accompanied by a friend or two, you explore the Muskoka waters as if you were one of the passengers from long ago. Indeed, in your mind's eye you can almost see the image of a moustached gentleman with a top hat on his head walking past you, an elegant woman in a flowing dress on his arm, shielding herself with a parasol.

Perhaps it's not your imagination. Whether you choose to enjoy your cruise in the ship's dining facility, in the grand bar area or up on deck, know that you are never really alone aboard the *Segwun*. The chill you feel is not necessarily coming off the lake. It might just be an unseen passenger leaning on the railing alongside you or a spectral crewman brushing by. The *Segwun*, you see, is a ghost ship, inhabited by spirits that have never bothered to disembark.

But the *Segwun* is nothing like the traditional image of a ghost ship as seen in horror movies and described in campfire tales. Far from inspiring terror, this vessel is one of the region's most spectacular tourist attractions. In fact, the RMS *Segwun* is one of the most iconic images of Muskoka, a graceful throwback to another era. Built in 1887, she's famed for being the last steamship in North America still fuelled by hand-shovelled coal and today offers peaceful voyages out onto the tranquil waters of Lake Rosseau.

Let's step aboard the historical steamship to paint a picture of its appeal. The first sight of the *Segwun*, tied alongside the dock, smoke spewing from the stack as the coal-fired steam engine warms up, is unforgetable. Although the ship is more than 120 years old, it looks as though it hasn't aged at all, such is the care of its restoration. Greeted by a uniformed porter, you venture across a gangplank and enter the ship through a portal in the hull. The horn blows to sound departure just as you make your way to the top deck and lean against the railing to watch as the ship pulls away from the shore. The rhythmic thrumming of the engines, heard and felt even several decks above, only adds to the feeling of nostalgia. Soon, the picturesque shores of Lake Rosseau, so typical of Muskoka—rugged rock draped by a dense green forest and lined with elegant cottages—begin to pan by at a leisurely three knots, and cameras begin to snap with frenzy. It's soothing and exhilarating at the same time, and it's not long before you realize why the *Segwun* is so beloved.

The *Segwun* is part of Muskoka's character, her very identity, a fond reminder of the steamships that were once the backbone of the region. In early years, roads were either rough or nonexistent, so steamboats were a vital lifeline delivering the mail and supplies that people needed. During winter, many parts of Muskoka were completely cut off, and people awaited the first plume of smoke from a steamship in

Watch out for the ghost of a dedicated crewman aboard the steamship *Segwun*.

spring to signal that the isolation was over. For summer visitors, the steamers were also the gateway to adventure. It took four and a half hours by train to get here from Toronto. When the train pulled up alongside the Gravenhurst Wharf, passengers could see the gleaming white steamers awaiting them, and they knew they had finally arrived in Muskoka and that their holiday had begun. For residents and tourists alike, steamships *were* Muskoka, and as the last of their kind, the *Segwun* occupies a special place in their hearts.

This timeless appeal may be behind the ship's haunted status. Is it possible that someone loves the ship so much that his spirit remains attached to it even after death has claimed his mortal body? Tradition says yes. The story goes that the *Segwun*'s century-old hull is home to a crewman of similar vintage, a resident spook said to be the spirit of a devoted former engineer whose wavering form has been seen throughout the ship, from the dark shadows of the cargo hold to the commanding height of the wheelhouse. The mysterious ghost is tied forever to his beloved ship, seemingly unwilling to entirely entrust her operation to other hands.

The *Segwun* was built in 1887 as the *Nipissing II*, after the original *Nipissing* burned to the waterline and sank. She was unique in that her hull was built of Welsh iron and was fabricated in Scotland before being shipped to Canada in sections, which were then assembled and riveted together in Gravenhurst. The quality of iron and construction assured the vessel a long life. Though the *Segwun* is today driven by twin propellers, in her original form she was an elegant side-wheeler. As part of A.P. Cockburn's Muskoka Navigation Company, she ferried passengers and mail to places all across the Muskoka lakes.

In 1914, the *Nipissing II* was laid up due to an engine breakdown and spent more than a decade tied up alongside the docks. It wasn't until 1925 that the ship was extensively refitted and put back into service. Gone were the distinctive side-wheels, replaced by a pair of propellers. Most of the upper decks were rebuilt, but the two lower decks were retained. With a new look came a new name: *Segwun*, which means "springtime" in the language of the Ojibwa who traditionally inhabited the region.

Two decades later, only two ships from a once extensive fleet—the *Segwun* and her sister ship the *Sagamo*—were still in service on the Muskoka lakes. The end of the steamship era was near at hand. Both the *Segwun* and the *Sagamo* stopped running in 1958. The latter was sold in 1962 and turned into a restaurant. On January 10, 1969, it burned and sank, leaving the *Segwun* as the last serving steamship.

From 1962 to 1973, the *Segwun* served as a floating museum, displaying memorabilia pertaining to the area in general and steamship history in particular. During this idle period, the ship deteriorated so much that by 1973 she was in danger of sinking. Recognizing that she was irreplaceable, the community sprang into action. Over a period of seven years and at a cost of $1.2 million, the heritage ship was restored by the Muskoka Steamship and Heritage Society. The *Segwun* has hosted a variety of passenger cruises, ranging from lunch cruises to sightseeing and fall foliage excursions, since its relaunch in 1981.

The *Segwun* has undergone a great many changes in the years since it was first launched, and it has seen Muskoka evolve from a wild frontier region to a summer playground and the heart of Ontario's Cottage Country. But one thing has remained consistent throughout: the ship's spectral engineer has refused every opportunity to disembark.

Kate Cox has served aboard the *Segwun* for 14 years, the last several as its bartender. She speaks about the vessel with obvious affection and points out that the *Segwun* has a near magical way of enchanting passengers and making them fall in love with it. Kate wasn't a believer in ghosts or the paranormal before she came aboard but has since had several head-scratching experiences that she chalks up to the ghostly engineer. Most of these are what she describes as "little odd-ball things," playful rather than unnerving, but they leave no doubt in her mind that the *Segwun* is indeed haunted by an unearthly crewman.

"Things are constantly and mysteriously being misplaced, especially my pen," Kate says seriously. "I'll put my pen down on my crossword puzzle and come back for it a few minutes later to find it missing. I'll search everywhere for it and not find it. A few minutes later, when I'm no longer looking, the pen will turn up where it originally was. Once in a while Visa slips will also disappear, which really freaks me out because like clockwork I put them in the same place. I'll turn around and then the missing slips are right back where they're supposed to be.

"You might think I'm just losing my mind, but I have witnesses," she says earnestly. "I was doing a crossword once when customers came over and distracted me from my puzzle. I needed my pen, but when I turned around it was gone. I turned the puzzle upside down, I searched the countertop, I searched the floor—nothing, it was gone. A few moments later I turned around and there it was, just sitting atop the crossword puzzle. I had customers witness it; they saw me searching for the pen and they saw it reappear."

Kate is convinced that the items disappear at the hand of the *Segwun*'s ghost, and she's equally convinced that the spirit is harmless and has a soft spot in his heart for her. He's merely a trickster, one who likes to make his presence known to her in a fun-loving way. Kate feels safe around him, and as long as she feels the ghost's presence she instinctively knows nothing bad will happen to her. Only once in all her years aboard, though, has the cheerful bartender ever actually seen the spirit.

"It was in the morning one day and I was alone in the bar area, getting ready for the first cruise of the day. The engineer had come aboard and was sitting at one of the tables in the bar. I saw him out of the corner of my eye, and I distinctly remember he was wearing a green shirt. I started talking to him, saying good morning and chatting away. He didn't reply, which I thought was weird, and when I looked up to say something else he was gone. I was completely alone. When I went to find the engineer and ask why he left so suddenly, I found he was wearing a white shirt and he had not been up in the bar. I later learned no one had come up to the bar, and there was no one on board wearing a green shirt either, so I believe I saw a ghost…I know I saw a ghost."

Kate isn't the only person to see the spectral engineer, and he must wander a lot since he has on occasion made his presence known all over the ship. An Australian woman enjoying an excursion aboard the historic vessel approached a crewmember and matter-of-factly informed him that the *Segwun* had a ghostly passenger. She claimed to have seen his misty form, distinct in detail and yet transparent, standing behind the vessel's wheelhouse. The woman couldn't have mistaken a passenger or member of the crew for a ghost because the area indicated is off-limits and roped-off, leaving one to conclude that she was either fabricating the entire experience or, incredible as it sounds, was actually telling the truth. The solemn and slightly bewildered look on the passenger's face left the crewmember to conclude that she truly believed she had laid eyes upon the shadow of someone long deceased.

Elsewhere, people will occasionally feel something unusual in the hold, a distinct but intangible sense of someone unseen watching them. The person might see a movement in the darkness, perhaps even catch a momentary glimpse of a face peering out from the shadows, and yet he's completely alone in the bowels of the ship. The individual is left shaking his head. A trick of the light? Maybe. Or perhaps something else, something unexplainable.

It's also said that the engine room has on occasion been the scene of unusual phenomena. One passenger claims to have seen several balls of light, of different sizes, hovering near the ceiling, and according to Kate, engineers over the years have felt an invisible presence while overseeing the steam-powered machinery that runs the ship. This technology is more than a century outdated, as foreign to modern eyes as a computer would have been to people from the 1800s, and very fickle. One can almost imagine the phantom engineer peering over the shoulder of his modern-day counterpart to ensure his beloved ship is in good hands and to prevent any harm from coming to her. It's a comforting thought, one that makes the tragedy of a spirit trapped in a realm where he no longer belongs somehow less painful.

The question remains: does the historical record offer any hints as to the identity of the *Segwun*'s ethereal crewman? While certainly there have been several individuals particularly associated with the *Segwun*, each of whom dearly loved the graceful vessel, one person stands out among the crowd. Captain Jack Ariss was a lifelong mariner who spent more than five decades aboard a number of ships. Some people would argue that he was more at home aboard a ship than on dry land. He loved life as a sailor: the serenity that comes with being out on the water, the challenge of facing unpredictable weather conditions, the daily adventure, the thrill of having a massive vessel answering his command. Captain Ariss spent 20 years as skipper of the *Segwun*, and even as old age crept up on him he refused to pass over control of the helm to anyone else—this ship was his!

On Labour Day 1956, 69-year old Captain Ariss was guiding the *Segwun* in from her morning cruise when a strong wind began blowing in behind him, pushing the vessel forward faster than anticipated. There was not enough time to reverse the engines to slow the vessel down, and unfortunately there was no one on the wharf to catch and secure the lines that could have brought the *Segwun* to a stop. As a result the ship grounded her bow in the sand along the shore. Captain Ariss was furious and left for lunch fuming over the incompetence of the wharf staff. His mood hadn't improved much when he returned a few hours later for the *Segwun*'s afternoon voyage. Still livid, he gently guided his beloved ship away from the dock. No sooner had the ship safely reached open lake than the skipper felt a sudden tightening in his chest; his legs buckled, and stars began to appear before his eyes. He collapsed at the wheel, suffering a massive stroke.

It was a close call, but Captain Ariss survived the attack. Unfortunately, he never fully recovered and remained partially paralyzed for the few remaining years of his life. Such was his love for the *Segwun* that, despite his limitations, he returned as nominal captain for a few cruises in 1957 even though he served more as an advisor than a real skipper.

Everyone who knew the old mariner knew that when Captain Ariss left the ship for the final time, he left behind a part of his heart and soul.

Is it possible then that it is his spirit lovingly remains aboard the *Segwun*, and that the story of a ghostly engineer is simply the result of an altering of the facts over time, details changing or being lost each time the story was told? Captain Ariss had to be pried away from the ship; over decades of service the *Segwun*'s wheel had become an extension of his arm, and her thrumming engines as familiar as the beating of his own heart. It makes sense that he would return to the *Segwun* after death.

The *Segwun* is widely recognized as a romantic symbol of Muskoka, offering passengers a chance to experience the elegance, nostalgia and heritage of the region's past. Thousands of people step aboard every year to be transported back in time to an era before highways, when steamships ferried mail, passengers and freight to villages, resorts and cottages across the Muskoka Lakes. Few of them realize, however, that an unseen figure greets them as they come aboard and protectively watches over them during the cruise, ensuring the ship and its passengers return safely. Rather than sail off into the otherworldly sunset as most spirits do when their mortal bodies die, this soul—Captain Jack Ariss, a former engineer, or whoever he might be—prefers in death to remain aboard the ship where he felt most at home while living. Anyone who has experienced the grace and romance of the *Segwun* can well understand: it's hard enough to pull oneself away after an afternoon cruise; to do so after a lifetime aboard must be all but impossible.

Jocko River Taint

The Jocko River, located near the city of Temiskaming Shores in northeastern Ontario, is a tributary of the Ottawa River that courses through some of the most picturesque wilderness in the province. The waterway has become popular with outdoor enthusiasts: canoers paddle along its length, campers raise tents along its rugged shores, and hikers venture into the primal forests on either side of it. It's a place of tranquility and solitude, a place where peacefulness seems to reign supreme.

There's a darker side to the picture, however, one most visitors thankfully never experience. This northern watershed is the focal point for enough Halloween-caliber stories to make any sane person question the wisdom of wandering into the woods alone. One story, probably told hundreds of times around late-night campfires, deals with the infernal spirit of a vile lumberjack by the name of Toussant who refuses to rest easy in the fires of hell. His ghost wanders along the length of the Jocko River, terrorizing anyone unfortunate enough to cross his path.

This chilling story begins a century ago. In the early 20th century, lumbermen poured into this wild and unforgiving region to harvest the bounty of the forests. Lumbermen were, by their nature, largely uninterested in the constraints of civilization. They enjoyed their existence on the frontier, free of the shackles of societal mores. Alcohol was a constant companion, and in their drunken hazes violent confrontations were common. To say that these men were rough around the edges would be a gross understatement, and yet most were generally decent, if unrefined, souls.

A man lost when he faced off with the devil during a springtime log run down the Jocko River.

But there were exceptions, men who hid amongst the fringes of humanity to escape the law and to indulge in the deepest excesses of behaviour without fear of persecution. A fellow named Toussant was one such individual, a black-hearted wretch who took to the woods after he had outstayed his welcome in more civilized areas. But while he could escape from his past, he could never escape from his destructive urges. The wicked lumberjack cursed, stole, fought, raped, conned and even murdered his way through countless shanty camps and frontier towns.

Indeed, Toussant was such a wicked soul and led such a depraved life that he eventually gained the attention of the devil himself. The lumberjack knew that his actions while on earth would eventually lead to the Dark Prince claiming his soul, and that he would consequently toast his toes in the fires of hell for all eternity. But that was all a far way off, he assumed. Toussant figured that his day of reckoning wouldn't come until he was an old man lying on his deathbed. He was wrong.

It came during a spring drive one year about a century ago. Logs cut over the past winter were rolled by the hundreds into rivers swollen by the snow melt. Lumberjacks, equipped only with long pikes and nail-soul boots, were tasked with herding the logs down the raging waterways to awaiting sawmills. Men would balance themselves precariously on the floating tree trunks as they raced downstream, jumping from log to log to free those that became lodged on rocks or along the shoreline. It was a dangerous job, and it was during one of these spring drives that the devil came to claim his prize.

Rather than take his true form, the devil decided to appear to Toussant as a huge, black wolf whose eyes blazed red with evil intent. Toussant was riding a log in midstream when he first became aware of the frightful wolf pacing him from the shore, and he instantly recognized its true nature. Toussant had never known the sensation of fear before. Even while navigating the most violent of rivers or fighting for his life in a drunken brawl, he had never known terror. But Toussant felt its icy tendrils working their way through his body now. He was too young to die. He hadn't yet had his fill of debauchery. He wasn't ready to be dragged kicking and screaming into the torturous heat of hell. And so he tried to flee.

Nimbly jumping from one log to the next, Toussant raced for the shore opposite the fiendish beast. He thought if he could put the river between himself and his hunter he might survive this day. Glancing over his shoulder, Toussant was horrified to see the great black wolf giving chase, effortlessly moving across the bobbing logs, almost upon him. Panicking now, Toussant pushed himself to greater speed. But desperation bred recklessness, and inevitably the otherwise sure-footed lumberjack lost his balance. Arms flailed wildly as he attempted to right himself on the slick log, but to no avail. Toussant fell into the cold, spring-time river.

Pulled underwater by the current, the lumberjack struggled against its grip and fought his way to the surface of the racing river. There, he came face-to-face with the coal-coloured wolf, whose burning stare was fixed hungrily on him. The creature was so close he could smell its horrid breath and feel its heat on his face. Toussant pleaded for mercy, begging the devil for just a few more years, but it had no effect on the great beast. Whenever the lumberjack reached for a log that might keep him afloat, the wolf would bite at his hand. Salvation was so close, and yet always out of reach.

The bitter cold inevitably began to sap Toussant's strength, and he found it increasingly hard to keep his head above the frothing waters. The wolf's fearful gaze never wavered from the man, even as the pull of the river began to drag him below the surface. The last thing Toussant saw before his body was condemned to the watery depths was the burning stare of the wolf. The devil had claimed his prize.

But Toussant's reprehensible soul may have escaped hell after all—at least for the time being. Over the years, numerous reports of people having run afoul of the lumberjack's spectre have been documented, with all encounters leaving the witnesses terrified and scarred for life. Toussant's temperament, according to most accounts, has hardly been improved by a century of narrowly avoiding brimstone and hellfire, the threat of which never recedes. In fact, he may be more driven by evil impulse than ever before, a malice-tainted soul seeking to torment the living.

When the night winds die and a light mist rises from the water, the dark figure that is Toussant emerges from the depths of the Jocko River. He appears as a man of dense, writhing black smoke. His blood-red eyes stare angrily at whoever is unfortunate enough to see him, and bony knuckles reach out from the dark void as if to snatch their souls. Toussant lingers on well past his horrifying death, seeking to spread his pain to the living. Even when he's not actually seen, Toussant's presence is betrayed by piercing screams ringing out in the dead of the night or by an oppressive sense of foreboding that clings to a person like a damp fog. In any event, an encounter with Toussant never fails to instil terror in the hearts of all present.

One eyewitness account comes from a camper who has asked that his name be given only as Dan. He, his girlfriend and another couple were seated around a roaring fire one night after a day of exploring the wilderness around the Jocko River. Dan noticed a sudden and inexplicable drop in temperature that caused him to huddle closer to the flames. More ominously, he felt a presence. He didn't see anyone, but he could feel hateful eyes boring into his back and an electrical current of fear racing through his body.

Dan tried to shake the feeling but couldn't. Then he saw the dark figure of a wild-looking man standing just on the edge of the fire's glow. Although he was human in shape, his body looked like a mass of churning black smoke and his eyes danced with coal-like embers. Dan averted his gaze, thinking he was seeing things, and when he looked back the figure was gone, but the eerie feeling of being watched wasn't. In fact, it remained with him all night. Even to this day, the malice he sensed in the spirit gives Dan cause to shudder.

Thankfully, such encounters between the living and the long-dead are rare. Toussant fouls the otherwise pure waters of the Jocko River with his hateful presence, and most people believe the blight isn't bound to be lifted anytime soon. After all, Toussant will do all he can to decline the formal invitation to hell that the devil extended on that cursed day.

Skeleton Lake Tragedy

The mist was rising slowly from the water, and somewhere out on the lake loons called to one another as the sun gently rose above the horizon and nudged awake those sleepy souls curled up in their cottage beds. But not everyone chose to sleep away one of life's simple wonders, the Muskoka dawn. One lonely fisherman paddled his sturdy canoe across the mirror-like surface, soaking in the peace and quiet. He chose to start his day by getting up bright and early before the rest of the world arose and shattered the tranquility with a chorus of modern-day noises. For him, the outdoors was his life. He enjoyed the smell of the lake, the vibrancy of the lush green forest along the shoreline, the churchly hush of the pre-dawn hours and the stillness of the water when no one else was on it.

As the sun brightened and warmed up the day, the fisherman couldn't help but notice a wavering image just ahead, lurking just beneath the surface of the water. The man paddled closer, leaned over the side of his canoe and peered into the depths. Hard as he tried, he couldn't focus on what he was looking at. Then, suddenly, the shape slowly began to surface and float alongside the canoe. What he saw almost knocked him into the water: a nearly transparent human arm, reaching up from below, waved gently in the water. He recoiled in horror, a scream echoing across the lake and shattering the morning calm.

The man took a moment to compose himself, and even gave his head a shake to clear his mind. *This can't be*, he thought. *I must be mistaken.* Cautiously, he looked into the water again, and the lake revealed its ghastly secret. There, before his eyes, were the skeletal remains of a woman with her boney arms entwined protectively around a young child. His breath felt heavy in his chest and he shrank back.

In near panic, the fisherman hastily paddled back to the safety of shore, fearing that he might be pulled in himself. Even more troubling, when he returned later with a companion to recover the bodies, there was nothing there. Had they settled back to the lake bottom, or did they simply fade away...

Skeleton Lake has had more than a few witnesses to terrifying phenomena similar to that experienced by this horror-stricken fisherman. Some even date back to when Europeans first arrived in the area in the 1860s. These newcomers to the region found a beautiful lake with deep, crystalline waters studded by small islands. But they also found something else: a pair of human skeletons. And therein lies the basis of the lake's haunting name. After all, an eerie name demands an equally eerie story to explain its origin, so it's only appropriate that Skeleton Lake should boast a ghost story of its own. Many people in area know the bare bones of the tale—if you'll pardon the pun—but few know the full story in all its painful details.

The men who, a century and a half ago, stumbled upon the grisly scene of two human skeletons were surveyors working on the north end of the lake, employed in laying out lots for future settlement. At the time of their startling discovery, they were simply walking the lakeshore when they saw, lying stretched out on the rocks, a pair of skulls and various other human bones. It was obvious that these bodies had been here several years, predating European habitation of the region. Horrified and yet intrigued by their discovery, the surveyors approached the chief of the local Ojibwa tribe one night and inquired about the bones.

The tribe elder eased down onto the ground beside a crackling fire. He clasped his weathered hands together and looked intently into the dancing flames. He had a faraway look and was deep in thought, allowing painful memories to slowly resurface from years gone by. The men were fascinated by his serious demeanor. They took their seats in a half-circle around the aged chief and waited, breathless, for the tale to begin. Finally, in a voice heavy with sadness, the frail old man spoke.

"For many winters my people camped along the lake of which you speak," he began. "The water was usually full of trout and the deer grazed in the nearby swamps. It provided a bounty that sustained us during even the harshest seasons. But one winter neither fish nor game was present, and my people were faced with starvation."

He shook his head slowly with the memory. "We had to move on in search of food if we were to survive. To do otherwise would be to die, slowly and painfully. But some of my people were too weak to undertake the journey. One of them was a 10-year-old boy. His mother, a courageous woman who had only recently lost her husband, refused to abandon her only child. He was her reason for living. So she did the only thing a mother could do. She stayed with her son when the tribe moved on, knowing that to do so would mean her death as well."

The chief left his trance-like state and momentarily looked up from the fire, only to be greeted with his audience of sorrowful men staring back at him. All were visibly affected by the tragic story.

"We left them behind, and soon the deathly silence of winter settled on the mother and son. Their fire eventually burned out, the cold crept in, and they held each other close as the life slowly drained from their shivering bodies. A mother's cry echoed through the woods, and then there was silence. It was their bones that you found. The lakeshore has become their eternal resting place."

The night grew silent and the fire slowly dimmed. The chief, his eyes heavy with sadness, absently tossed twigs into the flames. "Their spirits never left those shores. We call it Spirit Lake, and my people have refused to camp there ever since. When we passed by the lake thereafter, we did so in silence, afraid that we might awaken the spirits of the mother and son who still haunt the rocky shores."

The surveyors were grim-faced, moved by the tragic sacrifice of the woman and at the same time terrified by the thought of restless ghosts wandering the woods. They simultaneously began shaking with uncontrollable chills, instinctively knowing what the other was feeling and sharing the emotion.

These men carried the story away with them and would tell it many times over the following years. With each retelling its legend grew. Soon enough, nearly everyone in Muskoka had heard of the hauntingly beautiful lake and the spectral natives who lost their lives upon its shores. In time, this body of water became known as Skeleton Lake, the name a lasting memorial to a mother's undying love and devotion for her son.

Throughout the late 1800s, guests of Windermere House, one of the most popular resorts on nearby Lake Muskoka, would pile into horse-drawn wagons to be driven up to the shores of Skeleton Lake. They would come to experience the legendary clear waters, to fish from its bountiful stock and, of course, to be entertained on-site by the tale of the ill-fated Ojibwa woman and boy. There was something irresistible about sitting in the near dark out in the woods and listening to a spooky story designed to make your nerves jump and your flesh creep. It was a popular outing for Victorian-era vacationers.

At the same time, homesteaders began to settle the foreboding wilderness around Skeleton Lake, intending to cut down the trees and replace them with farm fields. Some of these people would tell of a spectral native woman who had been seen time and time again wandering through the forest, perhaps searching for her people. Sometimes she was merely skin and bones, frail and haggard, but other times she appeared drenched, her dress clinging to her body and her long black hair wet against her back. Others of those homesteaders would tell of a sorrowful weeping that could be heard carrying across the still waters of the lake. A few witnesses who dared to share their frightful experiences spoke of having seen a pair of skeletons floating in the water. The spirits of the long-dead mother and son abandoned by their tribe are still confined to the area in the vain hopes that their people will return to them.

Time passes, memories fade and stories are forgotten. As a result, few people today are aware of Skeleton Lake's fascinating history or the origin of its eerie name. Modern cottagers are simply aware that there is something special about this lake with its crystal clear waters, an intangible quality that binds one's heart and soul to it. Once you've been touched by Skeleton Lake you never forget it, no matter how old you get or how far away you go.

The Ojibwa sensed the magic of Skeleton Lake too. Prior to that terrible winter, they looked upon it with reverence. In their eyes, it was a magical wonder that held powers beyond mortal comprehension.

Skeleton Lake is a peaceful body of water, but the wind whispers stories from long ago as it rustles leaves in the nearby forest. If you listen carefully, you may hear a spectral mother weeping for her dying son.

Marilyn Monroe at Yesterday's Resort

On Sunday, August 5, 1962, a warm wind swept across the Mojave Desert and slowly worked its way into Los Angeles. With it came a rush of sadness that settled over a home in Brentwood. Here, in the early morning hours, the lifeless body of a beautiful blonde Hollywood sensation was discovered.

Marilyn Monroe was only 36 years old. She had died tragically and presumably the victim of suicide. She was found lying face down on her bed with a telephone clutched in her hand, possibly having used her final breaths to make one last, desperate cry for help. This sad scene marked the end of Marilyn's painful story. Or was it just the beginning of another chapter?

To escape the constant attention of the American media, Marilyn would frequently vacation in the quiet and stress-free wilderness surrounding the French River in Northern Ontario. Some people believe it was only here, away from the cameras of Hollywood, that she could drop the Marilyn Monroe persona and be simply Norma Jeane. Some people also believe she was so content here that her spirit chose to return to this site after her untimely death.

The French River is one of Ontario's most beautiful water-ways, a place of picturesque charm and rugged beauty. Crystal-clear waters lap against rocky shores draped with a dense expanse of vibrant forest, making for the archetypal Canadian wilderness experience. Overlooking this natural wonder, standing on rocky heights above the main channel of the French River, is the historic Yesterday's Resort, a tangible link to the earliest days of tourism in Northern Ontario.

In 1923, Canadian Pacific Railway officials were looking for ways to increase passenger service on the line from Toronto to Sudbury. So the idea of an elite tourist resort on the French River became reality. The resort offered accommodations in charming, rustic bungalows that featured modern amenities such as running water and electricity. Completely isolated in the virgin forest 340 kilometres north of Toronto, accessible only by railcar, the resort offered guests complete solace. Rates at the time were $5 per day or $30 per week.

The resort enjoyed many famous visitors over the years. In 1939, King George VI and Queen Elizabeth enjoyed dinner in the main dinning room, and by 1950, the resort had gained a reputation as a retreat for Hollywood celebrities seeking to escape the limelight. Clark Gable and Ray Bolger (best known for playing the Scarecrow in *The Wizard of Oz*) were just two of the actors who signed the guest book. By then Marilyn had also discovered the wilderness retreat and frequently stayed in chalet 15 while recovering from miscarriages, marital upheaval and stress.

Yesterday's Resort hasn't changed much since it opened. The main lodge is maintained to look as it did 50 years ago, and though the chalets are equipped with modern amenities, when you enter them it looks as if time has stood still. Instantly, you feel the warmth and nostalgic solitude of years gone by. The tiny decks speak of the many guests who have travelled in and out of the cabins. A sense of history is so tangible here that you can almost imagine starlet Marilyn Monroe relaxing in a chair, enjoying the soothing beauty of the area while escaping the demands of her fame.

It is believed that Marilyn Monroe returns in death to the place that was her refuge in life.

Marilyn was always filled with insecurities, the result of a troubled upbringing that left her emotionally scarred. She was born Norma Jeane Mortensen but was later baptized Norma Jeane Baker for her single mother Gladys Baker. Gladys, whose family had a history of mental illness, had a breakdown and was hospitalized shortly after giving birth to Norma Jeane. She never really recovered, so young Norma Jeane spent her life being shuffled from orphanage to orphanage, never feeling wanted or secure. When Norma Jeane was 16, her guardian, to avoid sending her to another orphanage, arranged to have her marry a man five years her senior. Reluctantly, Norma Jeane agreed. The marriage was predictably short-lived, enduring only four troubled years.

During this time, Norma Jeane caught the eye of a photographer who believed she would make an excellent model, and, on the basis of his encouragement, Norma Jeane left her home, her husband and her life behind and headed for Hollywood. With her dark hair now bleached blonde, a studio contract in hand and a new name, Marilyn Monroe, the original Blonde Bombshell, was born. She rapidly became one of the world's most recognizable movie stars.

Her success and fame were a double-edged sword. They meant she was always judged, and every aspect of her life was fodder for the media and gossip. It must have been difficult for young Marilyn to be the scrutiny of so many people in Hollywood circles. She was largely considered a figure of lust or scorn. She was a sensation, and everything she did was considered shocking: she loved too much, swung her hips too much. Even the clothes she wore were constantly judged. No wonder Marilyn sought an escape from things that were being written about her, whether they were fact or fiction.

Marilyn was accustomed to travelling incognito, and during her stays at Yesterday's Resort she would use the name Zelda Zonk. To complete her disguise, she also wore a black wig and, sometimes, old baggy clothing. She had learned early that she had to be more than one person to survive in Hollywood. But who was she really? Was she the ditzy blonde sex symbol Marilyn Monroe, or was she the frightened child Norma Jeane, caught up in the unforgiving world of the movies? To the world at large she was the former, but in private Marilyn was sensitive, vulnerable, down-to-earth and surprisingly bright.

People who knew her claimed she could turn on her Marilyn persona at will. But at the French River resort she could be who she really was: someone who just wanted to escape the pressures of Hollywood and enjoy the simplicity of rustic life. When Marilyn would arrive at the resort, she was always nervous and on the verge of hysteria owing to the pressures of celebrity. She needed the peace this tranquil place provided.

So perhaps it makes sense that even in death Marilyn remains connected to the resort, especially to chalet 15, the very cottage in which she habitually stayed. Here, doors open by themselves as though someone is entering, but there is never anyone there, and occasionally a perfume scent that cannot be accounted for hangs in the air. Objects will move of their own accord, as if someone unseen is rearranging the décor to suit her taste. And staff members cleaning the building often sense a presence in the room, a presence that they describe as feminine and gentle.

On occasion, guests have seen a beautiful blonde woman appear and immediately disappear in the cabin. Marilyn made a rare public appearance before an elderly couple in 1996. They had been married at the lodge in 1946, and when their 50th anniversary came around, the couple decided to revisit the place where they began their life together. As fate would have it, they stayed in chalet 15. One day, without warning, the apparition of a beautiful blonde woman appeared directly in front of them. She lingered for a second, looking about the cabin with a look of contentment on her angelic face, and then disappeared. The couple was convinced they recognized the ghost: it was none other than Marilyn Monroe.

Her spirit is not only felt in the chalet but also in the dining area of the main lodge. Staff members working in the dining room have often seen a slender shadow following behind them, a shadow that doesn't have a source. When pressed, the witnesses always say that they somehow instinctively know the spirit is female. Also, the silverware on the tables can be arranged to perfection, but oftentimes staff will leave the room and return to find the silverware has all been rearranged in their absence with no explanation. And guests, while enjoying the comforts of the lounge, will be surprised to hear the sourceless, soothing sounds of a woman singing.

At Yesterday's Resort many strange events involve coffee, which was known to be one of Marilyn Monroe's favourite drinks. On one occasion a coffee pot had been emptied by some unseen visitor, and in the kitchen the coffee maker has been known to start on its own. Back in chalet 15, staff will find coffee stir sticks repeatedly appearing on the floor even after they are replaced on the appropriate shelf.

Fred Rysdale, the down-to-earth father of owners Doug and Mike Rysdale, believes he has had several encounters with the Hollywood starlet. "It was a Sunday morning and I was in the lounge reading Terry Boyle's book, *Marilyn at French River*, when I heard the sound of shuffling cards," Fred remembers. "It was very distinctive, and I clearly heard four sets of cards being dealt. I said to myself, 'Who the heck is playing cards?' But when I got up to look, no one was there. I checked the dining room behind me and even out onto the verandah, and there was no one to be seen. It was really strange, but I'm certain of what I heard."

That was Fred's first experience, but it wouldn't be his last. "I wasn't a believer until then. I had to experience something to believe it. But I started to believe from that moment," Fred says. "In my second experience, I was leaning against a chair talking to some of the girls who work here. Suddenly, I saw the three rows of glasses hanging above the bar moving back and forth, tinkling together. It was around 5:30, or cocktail hour back in the day. The girls witnessed the phenomenon as well. Later, I discovered that many others have had similar experiences, always at cocktail hour."

Several other inexplicable events have occurred since then, some witnessed by Fred and the staff, others by guests who have no knowledge of the resort's haunting heritage. It's more than enough to make a believer of Fred Rysdale. He, like many others, now believes that whatever peace she found here brings her back time and time again to escape the glare of the spotlight.

Maria is a huge fan of the actress, and when she heard these stories she decided we had to go and see this resort for ourselves. It was her way of connecting with one of her favourite movie stars. We soon realized that Yesterday's Resort is a fitting name; in this nostalgic and historic setting, with its simple cabins and a lodge that reflects a bygone era, it seems appropriate to remember yesterdays.

"I had the opportunity to stay overnight in the chalet in which Marilyn vacationed so many years ago. You can't imagine how exciting that was for me," Maria recalled later. "The chalet was everything I imagined, full of rustic charm and yet comfortable. It has two bedrooms, but I found myself automatically drawn to the one on my left. Somehow I got the feeling that this was the one in which Marilyn stayed. It wasn't a guess; somehow I *knew* it."

That was just the beginning of Maria's connection to her Hollywood idol. "I walked around the chalet, sat in an armchair in the living room and enjoyed the spectacular view of the river below. It was breathtaking, and I began to see all the reasons why Marilyn escaped to this place. I was at peace. I actually had to stop and think if in fact these were my feelings, or were they someone else's? And I could swear I felt a presence in the cabin with me, an unseen person enjoying the tranquility just as I was."

Interestingly, our cameras refused to work within chalet 15. None of the photos taken, a total of perhaps half a dozen, turned out. And yet all of the pictures taken elsewhere, even from just outside on the cabin's porch, developed beautifully. A strange coincidence? Perhaps. But it left us wondering whether there was an unseen presence playing havoc with our cameras. Maybe Marilyn resented the use of a camera here in the one place she always turned to escape the public eye.

If the spirit that haunts Yesterday's Resort is indeed Marilyn Monroe—and many believe it is—then the tortured actress must have found here the peace and contentment she was desperately looking for in life and therefore refuses to leave in death.

Ghosts of Cobalt

History is everywhere in Cobalt, a small, one-time silver rush town in Northern Ontario. It's in the head frames that rise up from the rock like silent sentinels. It's in the gaping depths of mine shafts, from which so much valuable silver was extracted in years long past. It's in the ruins of mill sites and the rusting machinery that lies scattered about the terrain. And, if countless stories are to be believed, history also lives in the form of ethereal spirits and other mysterious monsters that lurk among the shadows of this hauntingly beautiful landscape. In 2001 a TV Ontario program called *Studio 2* named Cobalt "Ontario's Most Historic Town," and the Cobalt Mining District was designated as a National Historic Site in 2002. Some people would argue it may also deserve a nomination for most haunted.

"Hundreds died here over the years in the pursuit of riches, many in horrific ways, and many more suffered terrible injuries or personal tragedies. As a result, Cobalt is probably full of ghosts, I'm sure of it," says Dan Larocque. An authority on mining and the community's history, Larocque serves on the board of the Cobalt Mining Museum and operates Rockhound Adventures. His mind is full of facts, not flights of fancy.

And yet, he's certain of the existence of ghosts. "Go up to the Nipissing mine site as night begins to fall and look out over the town," he says somberly. "There's something creepy about it, an otherworldly presence tied to the town's tragic history."

That history began in 1903 when the discovery of rich veins of silver led to a Klondike-like rush that saw wilderness give way to a Wild West boomtown overnight. Fortunes were made here, and from 1904 to 1920, Cobalt was the richest silver producer in the British Commonwealth. That's the glittery side of the story. Delve into the dark recesses of the past, and another image emerges. It's an image of fire wiping out shanty streets, of cholera killing hundreds owing to poor sanitation, of harsh elements and brutal working conditions, and of almost countless deaths and debilitating injuries in the choking dust of unsafe mines. Cobalt demonstrated how mining could generate wealth and power, but also human misery.

By the 1920s, the silver was beginning to run out. Within a few decades, even the most stubborn of mine owners had to admit that diminishing returns no longer justified the effort. After the mines dried up, Cobalt withered; residents fled like rats from a sinking ship, leaving behind empty homes, boarded up businesses and so many shattered dreams. Within a few years only a few thousand people remained, and it looked as if Cobalt had one foot in the grave. But despite many grim years, the town proved too stubborn to die. Neither did the spirits of the past move on. Instead, many linger amidst the haunting head frames and darkened mines, reflections as faded as the town they call home.

The list of sites where tragic apparitions or anger-filled ghosts have been witnessed is extensive: the Silverland Motel, a one-time bank that dates back to the heyday of the mining era; the Colonial Mine, where tours are led deep underground through a former adit; and the Imperial Cinema, a former vaudeville theatre that may be home to a spirit who refuses to exit stage left. But without a doubt the two most haunted spots in Cobalt are the Right of Way Mine and the Fraser Hotel, and it is to these spine-tingling locales that we now turn our attention.

Right of Way Mine

The rust-streaked head frame of the Right of Way Mine rises from the rock like a ghostly tombstone of an expired industry, marking the location of subterranean tunnels long since gutted of any silver they once contained. It's now a local landmark and a tourist attraction through which local historian and rock-hound Dan Larocque occasionally leads tours full of eager visitors. The Right of Way Mine is also frightfully haunted. Dan will personally vouch for it.

For as long as he can remember, Dan had wanted to see one of Cobalt's head frames opened for tours. The Right of Way made the most sense: it was conveniently located just outside of town, it projected a moodily atmospheric exterior ideal for being photographed by eager tourists, and most importantly, it was structurally sound. A few years back, he began the process of making his dream a reality. The first step was an inspection of the building to determine what work needed to be done before people could be safely led through. He had no idea what he would find within the gloomy structure when first he opened its doors, but he certainly didn't expect to face his greatest fears.

Dan entered the building, abandoned more than 50 years, and swung his flashlight around the cavernous interior. Debris and rusting equipment lay scattered everywhere, and pigeons took flight from roosts high above. He ventured deeper, keeping an eye out for gaps in the floorboards but awestruck by the atmosphere within the structure. His footsteps echoed ominously, the sound rising high into the rafters 30 metres above.

"During this initial inspection of the head frame, I began taking a lot of pictures with my digital camera. It was strange because when I reviewed them later a thick mist and unusual orbs started appearing in several of them. And yet, I hadn't seen anything unusual when I took the pictures," Dan said. "I didn't think too much of it until we were up on the third floor and something started pounding on the floor below us. It was loud and sounded really angry, like a caged animal. Then it was banging on the windows outside. Remember, we were on the third floor at this time. Still, I looked out the window to see if anyone was out there, maybe someone throwing rocks, but there was no one. I also checked to see if anyone was inside the head frame with me, but there was no one anywhere. There was no explanation for what was going on, and it really freaked me out."

Dan believes the explanation for what happened that day lies within the Right of Way Mine's troubled history. In 1902, the Ontario government incorporated the Temiskaming and Northern Ontario Railway to run from North Bay to Cochrane as a way of opening up the Great Claybelt of Northern Ontario—a region of moderate soil in an otherwise inhospitable, barren region—to settlement by land-hungry immigrants. Construction of the ambitious line began the next year and proceeded quickly. The mandate for the railway included the mineral rights over a distance of 50 feet on both sides of the tracks. No one thought too much about this clause in the agreement at first, but when silver veins as thick as sidewalks were discovered in Cobalt in 1903, the mineral rights suddenly became extremely valuable. In 1906, the Temiskaming and Northern Ontario Railway leased their silver-rich strip of ground to a group of Ottawa businessmen for the sum of 50 dollars and an annual royalty of 25 percent of silver production. Thus was born the Right of Way Mining

The ghosts of miners who met untimely deaths continue to haunt the Right of Way Mine.

Company, one of the most enduring of Cobalt's countless mining operations.

While many of the mines in the Cobalt area were relatively shallow, the Right of Way plunged hundreds of metres underground and ran under the tracks for more than a mile. It was among the deepest mines in the area, the miners being ordered to venture ever-deeper by the greedy owners eager to extract every possible ounce of silver from their mandate. As a result of their obsession, over the course of five decades of operation, a fortune was extracted from the shafts that dove into the dark bowels of the earth. In total, more than 3 million ounces of silver at 50 cents an ounce were produced. In an era when an average day's wage was around one dollar, this figure represented great riches and made for many happy and wealthy shareholders.

Although the mine owners undeniably made their fortunes, the life of a miner was dangerous, unhealthy and largely unprofitable. Miners operated in a half-lit world, toiling on the edge of life and death. It was expected and considered acceptable in many mines to lose at least one man every year. If a miner didn't die from accidental cave-in, exploding gas pockets or flooding upon inadvertently drilling into an underwater lake or stream, illness was sure to eventually catch up to him in old age. Many miners were crippled by arthritis or rheumatism, wracked by a dry cough brought on by "black lung" or felled by lung cancer. To make matters worse, the mine owners invested no money in the town, so Cobalt (in common with most mining boom towns of the era) had nothing in the way of a sewage system. Raw sewage and waste ran down the streets to pool in low-lying areas and contaminate lakes and ponds, allowing illness and disease to germinate and run rampant. In 1907 alone hundreds of people died from cholera, and undoubtedly many deaths within the mines could be attributed to weakness or lack of focus among ill men who should have been in bed rather than slaving away with a jackhammer and pick.

Despite these dangers, miners grimly returned to the depths every day, fully aware that with each ounce of ore removed from the ground they were one step closer to depleting the vein and putting themselves out of work. Eventually the silver did begin to run out in Cobalt, and one by one the mines were abandoned. The Right of Way lasted two decades longer than did most Cobalt mines, but in 1953 its owners finally decided the then-meager gains were no longer worth the cost and effort involved. The Right of Way Mine closed; the head frame was boarded up; its miners were laid off.

Sadly, many miners who worked at the Right of Way never had the opportunity to seek out new jobs; more than two dozen men died in that mine over the years, and the abandoned shafts became their tomb. "During its years of operation, 27 men died in the mine," explains Dan sadly. "They died horrible deaths, and most of the bodies were never recovered because of cave-ins or flooding. The bodies of these men still lie beneath the Right of Way head frame, trapped forever within the darkness and cold. It's creepy to think they're still down there."

Not being able to recover the bodies filled the other miners with bitter sorrow. It was part of the miners' code that every effort would be made to rescue anyone trapped below-ground, even if it meant only bodies, not living men, were retrieved from the darkness. How does one look a widow or her children in the eyes and say there would be no body for them to bury? All they could do was gather in a church to pray for the victim and his family and seek solace from one another. Prayers weren't enough to alleviate the grief, however, and the losses weighed heavily on the miners who had to return to work shortly after each disaster, knowing that the tunnels they worked in were also the subterranean crypt for unrecoverable companions.

Is it any wonder then that many people who visit the head frame note that it radiates an unnatural eeriness and an unde-fined sense of loss and sadness? With so much death and despair surrounding it, it would probably be surprising to most of us if the Right of Way Mine wasn't haunted. Unusual sounds are frequently heard in the head frame, and the stale reek of decay wafts up from the depths below. Many people who take pictures here find strange things when they later review the photos—ethereal orbs, swirling misty shapes or dark shadows where none should exist. Others, like Dan himself, claim to be more directly and more horrifyingly affected by the paranormal.

The Right of Way head frame is now open for tours, which can be arranged at the nearby Cobalt Mining Museum. We wanted to experience the building for ourselves, and Dan graciously agreed to be our guide. Although we went in objectively, while exploring it we were not immune to the building's oppressive atmosphere. During our entire time inside the head frame, we experienced the distinct sense that unseen eyes followed our every move. It was an unsettling experience that had us continually glancing nervously over our shoulders and into the shadows. Stranger still, not a single one of the photos we took of the interior on either of our two cameras developed. The odds of neither camera producing even a single image seemed, to us at least, too much of a coincidence to be anything other than paranormal. It was also during this tour that Dan shared a second frightening experience that happened to him in the Right of Way head frame.

"It was the middle of winter, and my nephew and I came to the head frame to shovel snow for a tour bus that was due by later that day. My nephew wanted to see inside the building, so I took him in for a look around. When we got to the top floor, something started banging on the roof so loud and so hard that dust and loose nails began falling down on us like rain. I looked outside to see if anyone was there—maybe kids throwing things onto the roof—but there was no one around. And that wouldn't have made sense anyway. The banging was too loud and strong to be rocks thrown on the roof, and it sounded like it was originating from the inside of the roof, not the outside."

Dan pauses, the heaviness of the experience still apparent in his voice and demeanor. This memory is clearly a terrifying one that affects him even a year or two later. Dan takes a heavy breath and starts his story again. "While the banging was still going on, big, heavy chains that descend down the shaft into the mines started rattling and swinging back and forth, banging into the walls. These chains are thick and really heavy; they lifted cages capable of holding over a ton of weight, so you could imagine how hard it would be to cause these chains to rattle. Suddenly, a warm, thick cloud of steam or fog started rising out of the shaft leading to the mines below. There was no breeze, so I can't explain it, but it was terrifying. Then, just as suddenly, the steam seemed to get sucked back into the shaft and was gone. Poof, just like that, it disappeared. I've been in a lot of mines and head frames, dozens at least, but have never experienced anything like that. It wasn't natural."

At the Right of Way head frame, it seems the unnatural is the norm. It's a place where the weight of the dead miners is heavy in the air, almost tangible in its intensity. It's a place where unexplainable and often frightening phenomena occur on an almost routine basis. And it's a place where the spirits of the deceased cannot rest easily until such time as their bodies can be recovered and given a proper burial (which is sadly not likely to ever happen).

When we emerged into the sunlight from our tour of the Right of Way Mine, we gazed up at the head frame's towering shape. What an hour earlier had appeared proud and majestic now seemed cold, imposing and menacing. We began to see the head frame, and all the others like it around Cobalt, as more than merely historical structures. In our eyes, they were now memorials to the sacrifices made by miners in years past, many of whom lost their lives for the prosperity of mine owners.

Our time in the Right of Way also caused us to reconsider a ghost story we'd heard but cast aside as nothing more than folklore. Perhaps we were too hasty. Apparently, a headless ghost has been seen along the train tracks late at night, wandering aimlessly under the pale light of the moon. Since stories that feature headless spirits are so commonplace and usually baseless, we initially chalked this one up to urban legend or outright fabrication. However, during our tour of the Right of Way, Dan casually mentioned a well-documented incident wherein a miner was decapitated in the tunnels below—tunnels that just happen to run under the very railway line that this apparition is said to haunt.

The Cobalt of today is much altered from the town of the first half of the 20th century when the silver boom was in full swing. The mines are all gone now, the community has dwindled drastically in size and population, and many of the historic buildings have been consumed by a series of devastating fires. Yet, one still senses the presence of history here, and most especially at the Right of Way Mine. You cannot help but be aware that on this very spot brave men slaved away deep underground, in the dark and in unimaginably harsh conditions, lucky, in the end, if they emerged with a meager day's pay…if they even emerged at all.

And in case you need reminding of their sacrifice, and the fact that mining is one of the most dangerous jobs in the world, the ghosts of one or more of the 27 men who died here and remain entombed within the tunnels might just make their presence known in chilling ways. The Right of Way Mine is more than just a tourist attraction; it's also a shrine to the dead, and the ghosts are here to ensure we remain mindful of it.

Fraser Hotel

The building was just a shell, four stories of cavernous rooms and empty hallways. Footsteps echoed throughout, shattering the grave-like silence. Light filtered in through grime-encrusted windows, casting the interior in the eerie haze of sickly yellow light. There was something about the Fraser Hotel that screamed haunted, but when we visited it several years ago, ghosts and ghouls were far from our minds. We were there to record the fascinating history of this century-old building, and to see it as it was before planned renovations changed it forever.

While snapping photos of the decaying interior we happily listened while Dan Larocque, our willing guide, shared information about the Fraser Hotel and its unique place in Cobalt's history. The building was cold, stark and oppressive, like a sanatorium in some low-budget horror flick. Evidence of neglect was everywhere. Still, there was something impressive about it, and we were thoroughly engrossed.

Perhaps the planned renovation of the Fraser Hotel will cause the unhappy spirit who haunts it to move on.

We had gotten to the third floor when Maria stopped in her tracks. The hair on her arms stood up and colour drained from her face. A sudden drop in temperature—the air around her had turned icy cold—preceded the unsettling sensation of being watched by chilling eyes. "Is this place haunted?" she asked uncomfortably.

"It's funny you should ask that," Dan smiled, nodding. "A lot of people in town say the Fraser Hotel is said haunted. Let me tell you about it…"

It turns out that Cobalt's ghosts aren't just found within the oppressive darkness of the mines. They can also be found hiding in many of the town's historic buildings, foremost among them the foreboding, century-old Fraser Hotel. Among locals, this derelict building has a frightful reputation. The entity stalking its corridors and rooms is violent and hostile, taking out decades of pent-up anger on any unsuspecting individual who enters what it considers to be its own personal domain. Stories of its assaults are so widespread among the people of Cobalt that it takes rare bravery to push open the doors and explore the interior, and no one does so alone or after dark. Even when the foul taint of the ghost does not make itself known, an unnatural aura that pervades the entire building sets nerves on edge. Walls with peeling paint, broken glass crunching underfoot, ruined furniture cast aside by previous inhabitants, mildewed and lifting tiles and layers of unidentifiable grime add to the sinister, decaying atmosphere.

The Fraser Hotel didn't always evoke shudders and revulsion. At one time, it was undoubtedly the most impressive and attractive building in Cobalt, the pride of a community growing in wealth and confidence. In 1909, Cobalt was nearing the height of its fortunes; in that year alone its mines produced some 25 million ounces of silver, making the community the richest silver-producing area in the vast British Commonwealth. That same year, the building that today is best remembered as the Fraser Hotel made its appearance. In its original form, it wasn't a hotel at all. Instead, it was the Royal Stock Exchange, designed to facilitate the tracking and trading of the silver being pulled from the nearby mines. And while investors and stock traders were conducting business on the main floors, dynamite for use in the mines was being manufactured in a munitions factory in the basement.

A short time later, the building was transformed into a hotel, a luxurious establishment patronized by wealthy mine owners when inspecting their holdings in town. Several foreign dignitaries stayed here while touring the town that appeared across headlines the world over, and well-known European theatrical performers would call the establishment home when their shows made stops in Cobalt. The hotel was a swank place where members of upper-class society could feel right at home. No money was spared in its design and furnishing, and the hotel even boasted a purple-mauve glass sidewalk that was illuminated from beneath, a feature otherwise found only in the classiest spots in New York, Chicago, London and Paris.

But the glory days were short-lived. For many years the building served as an office space for lawyers, a bank and post office, and living quarters for local professionals. Then, as the town's fortunes flagged after the 1920s, the once-impressive hotel fell on hard times as well, and gradually, over the course of decades, devolved into a seedy tavern and hostelry. By the 1960s, the only patrons were the dregs of society who drank and brawled with equal passion. "We used to sit at the Staedleman Apartments across the road and we'd watch the fights at the Fraser," remembered Peter Larobie in *We Lived Life and Then Some: The Life, Death, and Life of a Mining Town*. "They used to throw guys through the doors; the windows would be breaking. People would come flying out into the streets. It was just like the movies."

The Fraser Hotel had become a mockery of its former self. It was at this time that the hotel's most infamous guest checked in to one of the rooms upstairs and made the faded and tired building his home. His name was Hermiston; no one remembers his first name, for few cared to know it in the first place.

Hermiston, you see, was a brutal drunk who, under the influence of alcohol, hurled insults and abuse upon anyone in his presence. Most people avoided him. His hair-trigger temper and violent outbursts caused widespread fear, and his drunken antics became an embarrassment for town residents. Hermiston's drinking binges lasted long into the night virtually every night, and it was only when his eyes were glassy and his speech slurred incomprehensible that he staggered back to his room on wobbly legs. Often he didn't make it, collapsing in a heap on the staircase or in one of the hotel hallways. There, he slept off the drink and the hangover that followed. People simply became accustomed to stepping over his body.

Hermiston fit the rough-and-tumble Fraser Hotel like a glove. It was his kind of establishment. The booze was cheap, the companionship rowdy, and there were always other drunks foolish enough to test themselves against his meaty fists. He loved nothing more than beating another man to a pulp and then roaring with laughter, a drunken braggart standing over his victim. For a man of such low character, the Fraser Hotel meant good times.

But the good times came to a sudden end one night in the early 1970s, and where the drunken revelry ended a legend began. This particular evening began as did most others for Hermiston. He burst into the bar and began ordering drinks. A shot of whisky turned into two, and then three, until he eventually lost count of the shot glasses he'd emptied. As the alcohol did its work, Hermiston became increasingly unruly. He slung insults at everyone within earshot and threatened to beat the tar out of anyone who dared cross him. It was well after midnight when the swaying drunk, suddenly feeling unwell, decided to call it a night and began to crawl up the stairs to his third-floor apartment. Each step was a monumental achievement. Hermiston had been intoxicated to the point of sickness many times before, but the feeling suddenly washing over him felt new and unusual, and even in a stupor it unsettled him. Something was wrong.

With great effort, Hermiston climbed the three flights of stairs and, leaning heavily on the walls for support, began stumbling along the third-floor hallway. He had made it only a short distance when a tingling sensation rippled along the length of his left arm, and he felt a sudden tightening in his chest. Sucking in breaths of air became an agonizing ordeal, and Hermiston's eyes widened and began to bulge from his head as the pain increased in waves. He staggered along the deserted corridor for a few more steps, then his legs buckled and he fell in a heap on the floor. "Help….me," he managed to gasp as his face turned deathly white, but no one was there to hear his feeble cries. In light of the manner in which he had abused almost everyone in town, it's doubtful whether anyone would have rushed to his side anyway.

The hallway began to spin before Hermiston's eyes. He made a desperate attempt to crawl, but his limbs gave out and the world blurred as he sprawled flat. Panicked now, he tried to call for help again but the words refused to leave his lips. The constriction in his chest tightened as blackness crept over his vision. He fought to stay conscious but felt himself slipping into the void. Hermiston struggled desperately to pull away from the darkness, then let out a final gasp as the icy hand of death beckoned him to let go. He died alone and afraid, struck down by a massive heart attack. His body remained where he fell just outside of his room until someone happened upon him more than a day later. Few mourned his passing, and some even breathed a sigh of relief that his reign of terror was finally over.

More than 30 years have passed since Hermiston's final drunken binge came to a sudden end. The Fraser Hotel currently lies abandoned and empty, the days when it operated as a house of ill-repute little more than a bad memory. Few people find reason to enter the dilapidated building, and the malicious poltergeist lurking within the shadows of the building, said to be the spirit of Hermiston, still surly after all these years, apparently likes it this way. He stalks unwary intruders, waiting for the perfect moment to spring upon and so terrify his victims that they flee the building in terror, never to return.

The Fraser Hotel is bedevilled by a variety of inexplicable and often frightening phenomena, including one notable occasion when phantom footfalls were followed up three flights of stairs and along the third-floor hall before stopping before a doorway to what was once a guest room, perhaps even Hermiston's room. The fact that most of the reported paranormal activity is centred upon the third floor where the old drunk died seems to support the belief that the angry ghost is that of what was an equally angry human being. Hermiston was clearly a troubled individual who led a life of sin, so it's not hard to imagine that his spirit would be unwelcome on the Other Side. Instead, he remains bound to the one place he felt most at home, the whisky-stained Fraser Hotel. Decades have done little to temper him, however, and he remains as ornery as ever. In fact, on at least one occasion, simply terrifying the people who dared enter the building was not enough for him. He had to physically attack them in retaliation for invading his space.

The assault took place in the autumn of 2008, when a crew of municipal workers was tasked with entering the Fraser Hotel and cleaning out some of the mounds of debris littering its rooms. Each man was well aware of the building's reputation, but none of them put much stock in it. After all, ghost stories were meant to frighten kids, and they were grown men. The only thing to fear about their assigned job, they were sure, was hours of tedious work. They could not have been more wrong.

Unlocking the front doors, the men began to lug their gear into the hotel. They paused momentarily to allow their eyes to adjust to the gloom and take in the ruined interior. They whistled at the state of ruin and decay. "What a wreck," they agreed, with a hint of sadness in their voices. Then they got down to business and started to remove the debris, carrying it outside to an awaiting truck. All went well until they started to move their equipment up the stairs toward the third floor. That's when things took a horrific turn.

The workers were sweating from the exertion, yet suddenly their arms goose-pimpled as an icy cold draft raced down the stairs and washed over them like an arctic wave. It was so cold that the men started shaking, and their breath came out like frosted mist. The lead worker looked up toward the third floor and his eyes grew wide in terror. A dark shadow, vaguely shaped like a man and floating in the air at chest height, appeared from the third-floor hallway and lunged toward him. Limbs of swirling darkness reached out in search of living flesh. The worker screamed as the wraith flew toward him, but his cries were cut short when it grabbed him by the throat with its black tendrils and started choking the life from him. Although the entity was incorporeal and transparent, its grip was like a vice, crushing against the man's windpipe and causing him to struggle for breath.

The other workers fought against a rising tide of fear that threatened to overwhelm them. They had never seen anything like this before, and it paralyzed them. Their companion was blue faced now as the vengeful ghost maintained its grip. Choking fitfully, the man managed to let out a horrifying scream that finally snapped his friends out of their terrified daze. They raced to his side, grabbed him by the arms and began to drag him down the stairs and toward the exit. The shadow held on for a second or two more and then finally released its deathly grip. Enraged at being deprived of the opportunity to finish off its victim, it went shooting back up the stairs, growling in anger. The sound was so unearthly, so filled with malice and hate that it sent each of the men into spasms of fright. The entity then raced down the third floor's main hallway, slamming doors, blowing sheets off beds and ripping the tattered remains of curtains off windows before vanishing.

The workers burst from the Fraser Hotel and into the welcome protection of the sunlight, each one shaking with fear and adrenaline. They struggled to catch their breath and looked at each other with wide eyes, seeking comfort in companionship, but it did little to ease the horror they all felt. What they had seen, what they had experienced, should not have been possible and it shook them profoundly. Perhaps they could have found a way to rationalize the whole thing as some sort of mass hallucination had it not been for the angry red marks on the neck of the man who had been attacked by the spirit. There was no doubt *they* were real, and there was also no doubt the marks were in the distinctive shape of human hands wrapped around the man's throat, as if another person—a very powerful one, at that—had attempted to strangle him. With physical evidence staring them right in the face and providing irrefutable proof, there was no way for the men to explain away the experience as anything other than what it was: a violent assault by a supernatural entity.

"These are big guys, tough guys who are not really afraid of anything, but they were pretty freaked out when they came running out of there," says Dan Larocque, who spoke to the workers shortly after their experience and saw for himself the bruising on the one man's neck. "It scared them so bad they wouldn't go back in there, and I can't really blame them."

Since that terrifying day, the Fraser Hotel has been sold. Plans are currently in place to renovate it as part of an attempt to revive town fortunes in the wake of Cobalt's designation as a National Historic Site. Over the coming years, the building will be transformed into a culinary school, a fine dining restaurant, accommodations for students with units of subsidized housing, and a new home for Cobalt's Bunker Military Museum. It's hoped that this project will breathe new life into the moribund community.

One wonders what the spectre of Hermiston will think of his solitude being intruded upon after so many years. It's not likely he'll be pleased. After all, Hermiston disliked most people in life and seems to like them even less in death. The question is, then, how will he take his displeasure out on hapless culinary students, residents and diners? How many will he leave quivering in senseless fear, and will he attempt to kill again? Only time will tell.

In many ways, the Fraser Hotel symbolized the rough and restless male energy of a mining town down on its luck, where booze and violence were used to distract people from the hardships of their lives. When the renovations are made, that era will finally be put to rest, its dark stain cleansed from the community. Perhaps the rehabilitation of the Fraser Hotel will also rehabilitate its restless spirit, or even send him on his way. It is possible. *Isn't it?*

For everyone's sake, let us hope so.

The Pink House

Most of us have at one time or another experienced something unexplainable—the feeling that someone else is present when we are alone, items that suddenly go missing and just as suddenly reappear, fleeting glimpses of a movement out of the corner of our eye—but because it happens so infrequently we dismiss it.

It's different for our pets. Most cats and dogs can instantly sense the presence of something unusual in a home, even when we're completely oblivious to it. Often things like footsteps in an empty building, a frigid blast in a warm room or even a distinctive smell that has no source will cause us to pause for a moment and then simply shrug our shoulders and carry on with our day. For cats and dogs, these seemingly minor events can be far more traumatic; animals have such supernatural instincts and acute senses that they often fear what we don't physically see.

For Giles Alldin and his girlfriend Stephanie, it was the unusual behaviour of their feline friends that started them thinking that there were strange goings-on in their newly purchased home in the town of Bracebridge. When their cats began acting strangely the young couple took note, and soon enough they reluctantly acknowledged that their home may indeed be haunted.

Giles is from Peterborough and has a passion for history. He thought he had bought his dream house when he took ownership of an attractive, pink century home located on Ontario Street. He certainly didn't think anything of the fact that the building sat between two of the most notoriously haunted locations in town: Inn at the Falls and the

Bracebridge Court House. Giles simply enjoyed the idea of owning a home, and for a guy who likes history, what better than a home that dates back to the town's early years?

The executive chef at Inn at the Falls, Giles is no stranger to being around haunted buildings. He used to work at the Sherwood Inn near Port Carling, a historical property said to be haunted by an ethereal woman in red, and of course is now employed at a resort rich in paranormal tales, but he never really believed in life after death. At least not in the spirit-returns-from-beyond-the-grave sort of way.

That mindset has since changed. Soon after moving into their home in October of 2009, Giles and Stephanie began noticing really odd sounds. Like many new home owners, the young couple began to make renovations and personal touches to make the home truly their own. It was at this time, as the work was being done, that the odd occurrences became more and more frequent, and their two cats, named Peanut and Solo, started to act strangely. It was as if a resident spirit was being disturbed by the work being done to the house, and as the ghost grew more active, the two cats became increasingly agitated.

At first, Giles didn't give much consideration to the inexplicable noises, brushing them off as the kind of sounds that old homes constantly make—the creaking of settling floors, the low groaning of old pipes, the wind whistling over aging shingles. But as the weeks and months passed and his two cats became more and more jumpy, his dismissal slowly turned to belief and suddenly he realized that he had a greater depth of paranormal experiences than previously thought.

Giles is very easy to talk to and immediately opened up to relate his stories. As he told one story and then the next, other events that he couldn't explain but had pushed aside suddenly sprang back into mind. Soon, what began as a trickle had turned into a flood of unnerving happenings.

"I don't get startled very easy, but when our two cats freak out it gets me nervous," he explains. "The cats will sometimes freeze and stare at the walls really alert, as if frightened by something only they can see. They'll just stare at the walls, unmoving, and you can tell they're scared. And you know how cats are startled and run off when someone is at the door? My cats will sometimes do that for no reason. Also, while they follow us everywhere, they simply refuse to go to the basement, which is unfinished and used only for storage—the perfect place for spirits to lurk about. They tend to hang back at the top of the stairs, and you can tell they're uncomfortable. It's strange."

Giles isn't alone in noticing this strange behaviour. His girl-friend has been alarmed by it as well. In fact, an unexplained circumstance involving the cats left Steph "really freaked out." On that day, she came home from work and decided to take a shower. When she got out, she went to the closet to pick out something to wear. She distinctly remembers leaving the closet door open. She then proceeded to go downstairs to feed Peanut and Solo. A short while later, when she went looking for the cats, one of them, Peanut, had gone missing.

Concerned, Steph went in search of the cat, but Peanut was nowhere to be found. And yet, she could hear the cat crying and could tell that she was frightened. Thinking that Peanut might have somehow gotten outside, Steph ran out into the yard, but still there was no sign of her.

In a panicked state, Steph did the only thing she could think of and called Giles on his cell phone. Luckily, at this point he was already on his way home from work, and as he was literally around the corner, in only a few minutes he had joined in the search. They could still hear the cat crying, but though Giles—like Stephanie before him—looked everywhere for Peanut, he still came up with nothing.

Exasperated and out of options, Giles asked Steph to retrace her steps from the time she got home. After looking once again in the bathroom, they headed into the bedroom and toward the closet, which should have been wide open but instead was shut. Giles pulled open the door, and with a terrible yowl, Peanut sprang out. She darted from the room, ran to hide under the couch and cowered there absolutely terrified.

For more than an hour afterward she refused to leave her hiding spot. When she finally got the courage to creep out from under the couch, she wouldn't let either of her masters even get near. "She was petrified. I've never seen her so scared," relates Giles. "I'm pretty skeptical about things. I like to have proof. But I can't rationalize how a cat could go into a closet and close the door on itself, and as a result I'm starting to believe."

Now open to the possibility of the supernatural, Giles began to recognize that there were things in his life—unusual experiences, strange sensations, odd coincidences—that he could no longer excuse. For example, occasionally he would feel the sensation of someone walking past him while he was sitting on the couch: a chilling, passing breeze. He searched everywhere for the source, still trying to find a logical explanation, but hard as he tried he couldn't find anything that could possibly cause the sensation. Giles even went as far as to patch a small hole in the wall, thinking it was perhaps the origin of the breeze, but even when the hole was blocked the sensation would continue. He still hasn't found a possible source for it.

The perplexing events within the historic house are starting to make the occupants believers in the supernatural. Stephanie is convinced that there are ghosts in the home and occasionally gets scared if Giles isn't present. He, however, feels he still needs more proof to be 100 percent sure of the paranormal, yet he freely admits he can't explain the strange occurrences in his home. The one thing both of them agree on is that they feel the entity in the house doesn't mean them any harm. It was probably just slightly upset by the renovations they made and their presence in a place it considers its home.

Just who is the ghost in Chef Alldin's house? No one knows. It's tempting to think that it may have possible connections to either the nearby court house or Inn at the Falls, but it's just as likely it was simply a former resident who lingers in its familiar surroundings. The ghost's identity undoubtedly rests somewhere in the shadows of Bracebridge's past, but as of now remains safely anonymous.

How much would it take to convince you your home was haunted? How long could you dismiss all unexplained occurrences, no matter how unusual, or try to rationalize them in your mind? Eventually, even the most rational among us would slowly begin to accept that there are things that just can't be explained naturally. We'd have no choice but to put aside our reason and simply follow instinct, accepting that the supernatural defies explanation and just *is*.

For Giles Alldin, that realization came slowly, over the course of several months, and thanks largely to the keen senses of his beloved cats.

Germania Ghost

A driver is travelling alone on a deserted stretch of country road late at night. He comes around a sharp curve and is forced to slam on the brakes to avoid running down a young woman walking toward him in the middle of the road. She is drenched from head to toe and shivering uncontrollably in the chill evening air.

The driver feels pity for the girl and stops, opens the car door and offers her a lift. She does not say a word but slowly nods her head in acceptance and slides into the passenger seat, dripping wet. She sits in silence, still shivering and apparently unable to warm herself, all the while casting sad eyes out the window. Her face is streaked with moisture, but whether she is crying or the droplets are merely water falling from her hair is impossible to say.

Reluctant to intrude, the driver doesn't ask what happened to her, why she was out on this lonely stretch of road at night and why she is soaked to the bone. At one point, however, he turns to check on his passenger and finds himself impossibly alone. He's shocked. Where did she go? Was she ever even there? He begins to doubt himself. But looking at the wet spot on the passenger seat leaves the driver no doubt that someone had sat there. In a mysterious moment, the girl was simply gone.

The story of a phantom hitchhiker, a beautiful young woman seen at night in the illumination cast by car headlights, is one of the most popular in folklore. Every town seems to have a local version. In many cases, these stories are undoubtedly just urban legend, entertaining stories passed down from generation to generation that slowly take on a life

Drivers along this road occasionally come across the spirit of a forlorn young girl driven to suicide nearly a century ago.

of their own. But we mustn't be too quick to dismiss them all. Some may be born out of historical fact, an actual event that provides a foundation for a creepy ghost story. For an example, we need look no further than Muskoka and the tiny hamlet of Germania.

Germania, as the name implies, was established by German settlers in the 19th century. The common language and ethnicity made the community unusually tight knit, and bonds were made even tighter by neighbours marrying into each other's families. Pretty soon, almost everyone in the village was somehow related to one another. The entire community would congregate as one in church every Sunday, join together to share in difficult tasks such as barn-raising and harvesting, and gather to celebrate joyous events like births and weddings. However, the closeness meant that any losses were felt with unusual severity and that scandals would rock the community to its very core.

Among the settlers who made up this village were Adam Dietz and his wife, Wilhelmina. In 1863, Adam and his wife left Germany behind and headed for Canada, hoping to make a better future for themselves and their children. After spending 30 years in southern Ontario, they headed north to Muskoka in the early 1890s. Germania reminded them of their home country, and they settled happily among their fellow countrymen and began the exhausting task of clearing their land and transforming it into a workable farm.

Adam Dietz was a hardworking farmer, a devoted father and an extremely religious and proud man. He wanted nothing but the best for his children, but he also required their respect and didn't want any of them to bring shame to the family. So when one of his daughters, an innocent, pretty girl named Minnie, caught the eye of a young man, and when Minnie seemed equally smitten, Adam became alarmed. Minnie was too young to be courted and was still needed on the farm to help her mother with the neverending chores. Adam did not approve of the developing relationship, and he let it be known.

Under no circumstances could Minnie continue to see the young man.

Minnie loved her father, but she couldn't be separated from the boy who had captured her heart. She ached just thinking about being apart from him, so the idea of giving him up entirely was too painful to even consider. Instead, they would sneak off into the woods to spend time together, always returning before anyone grew suspicious. Soon the stolen moments between the young couple turned into a full-scale romance. There were moments when Minnie considered admitting her relationship, but she knew her parents would be furious, and the fear of what they might do in retaliation kept her silent. She resigned herself to the fact that the passionate moments she and her lover shared together would have to remain secret ones.

It was just a matter of time before the inevitable happened. When she discovered her pregnancy, Minnie was thrilled. It might have been youthful naïveté, the belief that love could conquer the world and all its problems, but she was genuinely happy and was sure that all would be well. Minnie wanted this baby so much. It was a symbol of her deep and unconditional love for her man, and she was not having anyone tell her different. Yet she kept her condition a secret from her family and friends; her heart was filled with joy, but she knew that her pre-marital pregnancy would cause a scandal.

Minnie managed to obscure her growing belly from her family for several weeks, but when no one was looking she would gently rub her stomach and talk softly to her unborn baby. As time passed, she found herself enjoying the feeling of the child growing inside of her, and she dreamed of the future that was in store for her and the man she so loved.

However, it wasn't long before Adam discovered that his unwed daughter was with child. He was furious. None of his children had ever dared to disobey him before, certainly not in a manner that would cause such a scandal. He worried more about what shame this baby was going to bring to him and his family than he did about the well-being of his own daughter.

Adam's seething anger was evidenced in his horrible treatment of Minnie. When he wasn't ignoring her very existence, he was yelling at her so loud and long that his face would become a crimson red, or making dire threats that left her quaking in fear. Shunned by her father and in despair, Minnie tried to talk to her mother. Surely she would understand; she knew what it was like to have a life grow inside oneself. But there was nothing Minnie's mother could do to sway her husband's feeling. He was a strong man and his strictness was not to be challenged, not even by his wife.

Sadly, the abuse from her father only grew worse as Minnie began to show more and as the small community began to gossip. Word of the pregnancy spread rapidly throughout the tiny village. Soon friends and neighbours began to point fingers at the young girl, to stare at her when she walked by and to whisper terrible things about her. It was as if the entire world had turned against her.

Growing desperate, Minnie tried once more to talk to her father. With tears in her eyes she begged him for forgiveness and to accept her unborn baby as his grandchild. She tried to convince him that she would make a good mother, and that her man would make a hardworking husband and father, despite his young age. If they were allowed to marry and raise their baby, if they could only have his blessing, they would make Adam proud. Minnie promised, she pleaded, she begged. Adam said nothing as his daughter cried herself hoarse. His hard face betrayed no emotion. His dark eyes offered no window into his soul, if he even had one. He simply turned his back on his daughter and walked away.

Adam wasn't the only man to turn his back on the despondent young woman. With it now apparent that their families would never accept their relationship, the man that Minnie so loved, the man with whom she had wanted to start a life, decided to abandon her. He simply couldn't handle the town gossip that painted him as a villain, and he didn't know of what kind of violence toward him Adam Dietz would be capable. Rather than face the consequences of his actions, the father of Minnie's child fled town. Like a coward, he left the young girl to deal with the situation all on her own: the physical changes resulting from a progressing term, the emotional toll of being pregnant and alone, the scorn of family and friends and the fear of her uncertain future. It was too much weight for a young woman, a girl really, to bear on her own, and her strength began to weaken.

Minnie no longer had the will to fight the battle around her. She considered the baby growing inside her a gift, but everyone else saw her pregnancy as a curse. Feeling so incredibly miserable during what should have been a happy occasion in her life, she found herself walking toward Weissmuller Lake one day with the quiet certainty that there was but one way out of her misery. She stood on the shore and looked out upon the smooth surface of the small lake. She had always found a sense of peace in its clear waters, and once again that familiar calming sensation came over her. Abandoned by everyone who had ever meant anything to her and no longer able to live with the scorn, she walked forward into the water. Tears filled her eyes as she softly talked to her unborn child and asked for forgiveness.

The water was cold as she slipped deeper and deeper into the lake. She held tight onto her round belly, but whether it was to comfort herself or the baby growing restless within it she couldn't decide. Minnie turned to look one final time in the direction of the small hamlet she called home, then closed her eyes and allowed the water to swallow her into its depths. She sank to the bottom, dying alone in the darkness.

A few days later, Minnie's body was discovered and pulled from the lake. Apparently unsatisfied with having driven the girl to suicide, the people of Germania added insult to injury when they decided that because she had taken her own life, Minnie could not be buried in the consecrated ground of the Lutheran cemetery. Instead, she was interred in an unmarked grave in an unrecorded location, shunned by her family in death as she had been in the final months of her tragic life. The poor girl's soul was denied a final peaceful rest.

Not long after her death, travellers began reporting strange occurrences along Germania Road from time to time. They still do. Germania Road remains very much as it was a century ago when despondent Minnie Dietz walked along it on her way to ending her life in the waters of Weissmuller Lake. A lonely stretch of road, it's the ideal place for the spirit of a young woman cast out by family, friends and neighbours to haunt.

Although appearances are blessedly rare, Minnie is sometimes seen walking the road, soaked to the bone and with a sad look etched on her face. She appears suddenly in the beam of a car's headlights in the dark of the night, causing the startled driver to slam on the breaks or swerve to avoid her. She has pale skin, wears a soaking wet, old-fashioned dress and is sometimes reported to be faintly transparent. Distant crying can be heard in the still evening air, cries for the child she killed during her moment of weakness. Witnesses who have come face to face with Minnie's forlorn spirit say they can see anger in her eyes and that they feel a wave of terror as she walks toward them. The horror lasts mere moments, for Minnie is there one moment and gone the next.

By all rights, Minnie Dietz had suffered enough under the abuse of her father and the cruel gossip of her neighbours. She deserved a happy afterlife. But the sound of her crying and the sad look on her face is proof that the passing of 100 years has done little to mend her broken heart. Still needing the support of her family and the acceptance of her community, Minnie continues to walk along the road near Weismuller Lake, searching for the love and the comfort of warm arms to hold her for eternity.

Ghostly Graves

On the night of a full moon, a young girl who so desperately wanted to join a popular circle of friends found herself in a field surrounded by a dense forest. Trees creaked as the wind howled through them, dark clouds overhead hung low with the promise of a storm, and in every dark shadow the girl envisioned lurking monsters. The cool October air cut through her jacket, causing goose bumps to break out on her body, but she tried to muster the courage to quell the fear rising within her.

Suddenly, the cemetery that was her destination was in front of her. Panic started to set in. The headstones were moss-covered and old, and the grounds looked unkempt. Trees had sprung up between plots, their barren branches reaching out like the arms of skeletal predators desperate for fresh victims. The moonlight, when it found a way through the clouds, created an eerie glow over the cemetery. It was as if no one had been there for years…no one living, at least. The girl's test was to find the oldest grave, read the name out loud to the other girls waiting in the distance, and then sit at the headstone for an hour to prove that she wasn't afraid. Only then would she be welcomed into the group of friends to which she so wanted to belong.

This test of courage occurred in an ancient and derelict pioneer cemetery in Muskoka but easily could have taken place nearly anywhere. Braving a cemetery after dark is a common challenge among young people, a cruel rite of passage, for we have an almost morbid fascination with cemeteries. Since time began, when a life ended we would lay the body to rest in a somber place that could be visited.

Folklore and frightful legends surrounding these burial places soon emerged, and before long, cemeteries were thought to be home to ghosts and ghouls. In today's society we even decorate our front lawns as cemeteries on Halloween.

Cemeteries are meant to be a reminder of lost ones. They are a place where lives are commemorated, where families are reunited and where we pay tribute to those who have left us. But have they really left? It's a question that has long tormented us. Some people believe that a cemetery is an unlikely place to find ghosts. Why would lost souls want to linger around such a depressing, lifeless place when they could return to their former homes? Others think that cemeteries do hold the spirits of the dead in their grasp. Ghosts are often reportedly seen and felt by people who go to a cemetery to pay respect to their dearly departed. In fact, many believe that cemeteries are charged with paranormal energy.

Perhaps the young girl visiting the unspecified Muskoka cemetery that moonlit night debated this question while she weaved her way amongst the tombstones. She hugged herself tightly and walked on shaking legs. With each step taken, she ventured deeper into the eerie graveyard and farther away from the comfort of her peers. After achingly long minutes, she found the oldest grave, called out the name as instructed and sat beside the cold stone, waiting for the endless hour to pass. Maybe it was the breeze, but she felt as though a cold hand ran down her spine. She squeezed her eyes shut and clamped a hand over her mouth, stifling a scream of terror. She was determined that fear would not claim her tonight. She was going to be brave even if it killed her. "It was just the wind; there's nothing to be afraid of," she reassured herself, not quite sure if she truly believed her own words.

Should you wander into a cemetery, beware the ghosts you may be disturbing.

As minutes passed, the moonlight started to play tricks on her eyes. She began to see shadows moving, figures looming in the darkness and monsters dwelling behind every tree. "Who's there?" she cried out hoarsely. It felt almost as if the words didn't want to leave her throat. The fear she had been unwilling to acknowledge rose from within to greet her. She wanted to run back to her group, but when she tried to rise to her feet, her legs froze. Her body had become paralyzed with terror, literally frozen in fear at the sight in front of her. She was a sensible girl, and ghosts, she had long ago convinced herself, didn't exist. But there, before her eyes, stood one. A black cloak with a hood floated toward the young girl. This was no shadow or trick of the moon. This was something horribly real.

The girl summoned all her courage, trying desperately to shake off the freezing horror that gripped her body. She tried to climb to her feet, to run from the undead horror stalking toward her, but still she remained paralyzed. Just then a bony hand stretched out from the cloak's sleeve, and an ear-piercing scream escaped her throat. She had nothing to prove to anyone. Her only concern was to run for her life, and at last her body obeyed. She ran. She ran faster than she had ever run before. Her feet couldn't move fast enough as she flew past the other girls waiting in the field. They had heard her scream and were laughing hysterically, convinced she had been simply spooked by the night.

Their laughter came to a sudden stop when they looked up and saw the black-cloaked apparition emerge from the dark-ness, malevolence burning in its hate-filled eyes, bony, claw-like hand reaching out to take hold of them. Then they too ran, each girl racing as fast as her legs could take her, too afraid to even look back to see if the spectre was following. Each girl was certain that at any moment a withered hand would take hold of her and that she would become the victim of the fiend's morbid hunger for the living.

But no hand clawed their flesh, and the creature merci-fully did not overtake them. When they reached the safety of the road and their vehicle parked there, they found the first girl waiting, shaking like a leaf, still terrified and begging to leave. There was no argument; the girls piled into the car and, with gravel spraying behind them, sped away. None of them had believed in ghosts when they left for the woods that night, but they all left absolutely convinced that ghosts were frighteningly real and promised that from that day forward they would leave the dead to rest in peace.

It's a terrifying tale, all right, and one we're assured is absolutely truthful. Even the smallest pioneer cemeteries are the resting place for dozens of souls; there's bound to be one that was sad, angry, tortured or victimized enough in life to reject its grave and return as a malicious phantom bent on terrorizing the living. Such a spirit would be, as the girls describe, twisted into something horrifying.

And yet, no matter how many eerie, or even downright petrifying incidents occur in cemeteries, people still feel the need to experience the thrill of visiting them after dark, preferably during a night of the full moon. It's tempting fate, but perhaps therein lies the intoxicating thrill.

Dwight Cemetery

While cemeteries take on a forlorn, eerie cast under the cover of darkness, spectral sightings and paranormal experiences are not limited to the hours between sunset and sunrise. Even in the brightness of day, when thoughts of ghosts and ghouls are far from people's minds, the dead can stir in their earthen graves. What begins as an innocent visit to a cemetery can quickly become something decidedly more. These next three ladies got more than they bargained for when, on a lark, they decided to venture into a small, local cemetery. What occurred troubles them to this day.

A few years back, Laura invited her friend Carol to spend a few days as her guest at her home in Dwight, a beautiful village on the eastern shore of Lake of Bays. On a seemingly normal afternoon they decided to take a walk around the community, accompanied by Laura's sister Linda. Carol had never before seen the area, so a stroll through the hamlet seemed like a great way to introduce her to Dwight's charms. As day turned to evening, they found themselves approaching the local cemetery and decided to enter, "just to check out the headstones," as Laura related.

This cemetery is very old, and few people have been buried there in recent years. Its long history made exploring it much more interesting. Many of the aged headstones were crumbling and barely standing, leaning precariously, almost as if they'd grown weary. Most of those stones were so badly worn that the inscriptions were no longer readable. Sometimes a name or a date could be made out, other times virtually nothing. The three women read those few stones that were legible, piecing together the lives of people long dead, stumbling upon ancestors of families still living in town.

Laura began to walk toward one particular headstone that caught her eye. She noticed that the stone had sunk down and was almost being swallowed by the ground. Despite the fact that the stone was worn with age and was partially submerged, the women were able to make out the name Emily on the headstone. They wondered about the person in the grave, how Emily had died, what kind of life she had lived. Did she die young, or did she live long enough to marry and have children of her own? What hardships did she endure settling this harsh land? Was she related to a friend or neighbour in Dwight? The three women left the cemetery filled with curiosity.

Sometime after Carol had returned home, Laura decided to visit Emily's grave once more. She went directly to the area where they had seen the headstone, but oddly she wasn't able to find the grave she so desperately wanted to revisit. She was certain she knew where it had been, but it wasn't there. Figuring her memory must be off, she began to wander the cemetery, going around to all the graves, searching for Emily's stone. As hard as Laura tried, Emily's grave was nowhere to be found. The graveyard is quite small, so she knew she couldn't have missed it. The headstone had simply disappeared.

Laura was stunned. Had both Linda and Carol not also seen the stone, she would doubt her sanity. But they *had* seen it. The grave *had* been there. All three agreed. And yet, Laura couldn't find it that day, nor could she during several subsequent visits. Emily's headstone, the entire plot, any hint of her existence, had simply vanished.

This is the only time, in all our years researching paranormal phenomena together, that we have ever come across a story such as this one. We've heard about many haunted graveyards (though they are less common than you might think; ghosts are far likely to return to their place of death or somewhere they frequented in life than they are to haunt their gravesite), but a phantom grave is exceedingly rare, perhaps even unique.

One can't help but wonder whether this was Emily's way of seeking remembrance. Unable to speak of her own accord, the timeworn headstone that bears her life's record would be the only means of communicating with the living. Unfortunately, this marker had either long since crumbled away or been swallowed whole by the ground, leaving Emily voiceless and forgotten. Perhaps when she became aware of mortal visitors to the cemetery, she decided that rather than appear herself and risk frightening the three women, she would expend her energy in making her tombstone materialize. Even if the stone remained only for a short time, it would be enough to ensure her name would not be entirely forgotten, even if the details of her life were.

Falkenburg Cemetery

In many ways, the tiny cemetery sitting alongside Moore Road is in direct contrast with the town it once served. Falkenburg Junction was once a thriving community but is today abandoned and forgotten, one of Cottage Country's numerous ghost towns. Unlike the former town lots, which are overgrown with trees and shrubs, great care has been lavished upon this final resting place for the men and women who lived and died here—some under tragic circumstances—so many years ago. Many tombstones are faded, others have fallen or become obscured by foliage, yet it's clear that people still hold this cemetery in reverence.

And rightfully so, for the headstones represent a history of the lost community and its residents, a record of yesteryear that will remain for as long as the granite weathers the elements. These stones, for example, tell us that Falkenburg Junction was born from the determination and enterprise of the Moore family, in particular town founder Matthias Moore, who settled here in 1874 and quickly established a thriving farm and then a sawmill that sustained not only his family but also the village that grew up around the mill. But while Moore had hoped there were great things in store for Falkenburg Junction, fate had other plans. When the railway came through a few years later, it built its station two miles to the south, where a new village, Falkenburg Station, took root. Old Falkenburg became a backwater and, eventually, a ghost town.

Despite its serene appearance, Falkenburg has its share of mystery. People walking near the burial ground have reported seeing a mysterious light glowing amidst the headstones like an eerie jack-o-lantern. Of course, when they move in to investigate, the orange glow simply vanishes. Once, a lit candle mysteriously appeared atop a gravestone as if it was placed there by a phantom hand. The individual who witnessed the event claims the candle and its flickering flame literally appeared in the time it takes to turn one's back—not there one minute, there the next. He doesn't remember the name engraved on the headstone but recalls it being feminine.

More ominously, another man visiting the cemetery felt an odd presence, a distinct feeling that he wasn't truly alone. He looked around, peered into the trees, even walked back to the road and glanced both ways. There was no one to be seen, which isn't at all surprising considering how out of the way the one-time village is. But even though the man could see that he was the only living soul around, the odd sensation of being watched and even scrutinized persisted. That's when he began to wonder whether there was an invisible individual, a non-living soul, with him in the cemetery that day. As if in answer, he felt a sudden, sharp pain at the base of his neck, like someone was running sharp nails across his skin. When he looked later, the startled witness found distinct scratch marks there, red and sore, having almost drawn blood. He was more pained, however, by the thought that he had inadvertently done something to disrespect the dead resting in the burial ground, thus causing their anger.

It's always rewarding to put a face and a background story to a haunting, but in a cemetery crowded with tombstones, all pleading with us not to forget the deceased they mark and each one identifying a potential ghostly suspect, the individual cry is often lost in the chorus. Even trained mediums have a difficult time honing in on one voice, one restless soul. But in the case of the Falkenburg cemetery, one possible candidate for the hauntings—if indeed there is only one—has been put before us, and when her tragic story is known, one can begin to understand why she might be resentful of the living.

Jane Samways was born on July 16, 1857, and at the age of 18 she married Francis Moore, the eldest son of Matthias Moore. Jane was a dutiful wife. She followed her husband when he decided to leave England and settle in the wilderness of Muskoka, far away from her family and the life she knew. She worked tirelessly alongside Francis, clearing away the brush that covered their homestead and turning the rock-filled soil to prepare it for cultivation. She cooked, she cleaned and she made their primitive cabin a home. Amongst all this toil, Jane somehow found the strength to bear Francis three healthy children. She did all a man could ask of a wife.

When Jane became pregnant again in 1881, her once-vigorous health had been worn down by multiple childbirths, years of hard work and the hardships associated with living on the frontier. As fall turned to winter and the pregnancy progressed, the expecting mother was confined to bed more and more. Jane did her best to maintain a cheerful and calm demeanor for her children, but she was scared for herself and her unborn child. Her fear was justified. On December 10, 1881, Jane gave birth to a stillborn baby girl, Florence Jane. Later that day, the exhausted mother died as well. She was only 24 years old and left three young children without a mother's love.

Francis apparently took her death hard. He became increasingly irritable and began to have heated arguments with Matthias over the running of the mill. Finally, something in Francis snapped, and he simply upped and left, heading for Toronto and a new life. He abandoned his children and never returned for them. Friends and neighbours were stunned. Taking a new mate was one thing, but abandoning his children to do so was considered seriously disrespectful of Jane's memory. More important than town gossip, though, was the impact that the loss of both parents must have had on the three surviving children. The pain must have been terrible.

Did Jane return from the grave in an attempt to be closer to her children, to give them the love and support of at least one parent? Was the trauma of her sudden death, which literally pulled her from the embrace of her little ones, enough to keep her spirit from crossing over to the other side? Does she rest uneasily because of the casual manner in which Francis cast aside her memory and turned his back on all they had built together in their marriage? All are plausible explanations; indeed, if in fact Jane Samways Moore does haunt the Falkenburg Cemetery, she may linger on because of a combination of all of these powerful emotions.

Her suffering left a legacy of loss and devastation in the very soil in which she was buried, infusing the cemetery with paranormal energies. It appears as though time has not yet begun to heal her wounds, because some people who come to pay their respects to the dead still occasionally experience things that defy explanation.

Cemeteries are intended to be a place of peace and tranquility for the deceased, where testimonies of devotion, pride and remembrance are carved in stone to pay warm tribute to the life—not death—of a loved one. But despite our best efforts to ensure that they are treated with respect and dignity, the dead don't always rest peacefully. Sometimes, their spirits claw their way through coffin and soil, bursting forth into a world that is no longer theirs. So as tempted as you might be, stay away from cemeteries after dark.

Ghost Wagon of Parry Sound

The full moon hangs low behind the trees, its pale blue light washing over the dense forest and casting eerie shadows everywhere. The woods are disturbingly silent and still; animals hide in fear, somehow sensing that something unnatural is afoot. Suddenly, the oppressive silence is shattered by the sound of wagon wheels rolling over broken terrain, chains rattling and old wooden boards creaking. You might even hear leather reins snapping on a pair of horses' hides, followed by snorting and whinnying as a whip lashes the horses' backs. A lump settles in your throat, and as hard as you try to make sense of what you hear, to rationalize it away, you realize there is no possible rhyme or reason for this noise that haunts locals in the vicinity of Dollar's Lake.

This strange phenomenon has been heard on moonlit nights many times over where the lake empties over Dollar's Dam into the Pickerel River. People whisper to each other, almost in fear of being overheard and ridiculed, that in the shadow-filled forests they've seen the glowing and almost transparent shape of a ghost wagon and its team of spectral horses rattling through the woods before suddenly disappearing along the water's edge.

Dollar's Lake is located just west of Port Loring, in northern Parry Sound District, and is a popular destination for campers, canoers and hikers. But along with this crystal-clear lake, you may get more than you bargained for, something out of time and no longer part of this world. If by chance you happen to find yourself in the woods on a bright-lit night of the full moon, listen closely for the sounds of a weather-worn wagon being pulled by an ageless team of stallions. An undead driver sits atop the wagon, his ethereal hands snapping the reins, his mouth opening to holler commands but making no sound. This chilling apparition is known to locals as the Wild Wagon, a tragic ghost from the long-past logging era.

The spectral wagon and its straining horses make an eternal journey along the overgrown Thirty Mile Road, lurching over rocks and through woods, continuously reliving a job of long ago. It's a journey that reminds us of something all too often forgotten in modern times: Cottage Country was developed not only by the hardy settlers who made homes and communities in the wild north, but also by the teams of horses struggling to pull wagons over treacherous terrain or straining to plow rocky soil, helping their masters to build a future.

The hardest working horses were those belonging to the logging companies. In the summer they pulled supply wagons and during the winter they dragged massive loads of logs through the snow-covered forests. The work was exhausting, and horses often had to be retired prematurely owing to the cumulative toll on their bodies. Some horses didn't survive long enough to be put out to pasture, meeting premature ends as a result of accident or injury. Such was the fate of the horses that pull the Wild Wagon, materializing nightly in a vain attempt to complete their ill-fated final ride along the no-longer-used Thirty Mile Road and disappearing with the dawn, still well short of their destination.

Although almost entirely overgrown today, the Thirty Mile Road was at one time very important to the region. It was built around 1880, through the forests and over the rocks in Blair and McConkey townships to supply and service the operations of the Ontario Lumber Company. The road was the lifeline of the company, providing its far-flung lumber camps and their annual logging drives with food and fodder, mail and other necessities. In October, it swarmed with "shanty tramps" (as lumberjacks were often known throughout the region) looking for a winter's work in the camps. A busy thoroughfare, it ran from Port Loring west to Kidd's Landing on the Pickerel River. Steamboat service completed the link from Kidd's Landing to the company sawmill at Copananing, where the main outlet of the French River enters Georgian Bay. About 10 miles out of Port Loring, the road passed through the farm and buildings of the company's inland depot where supplies were stored, horses were pastured over summer and the company manager made his headquarters. Legend says that the Wild Wagon began its final ride from this long-gone depot.

The sun had hardly risen in the morning sky when the driver set off in his wagon, bound for Port Loring where he would gather supplies for one of the logging camps operating in the area. The trip was uneventful but, because the Thirty Mile Road was in fact little more than a rough, rutted trail, the driver arrived in town tired and aching. Although desperate for refreshment, he dared not head for the hotel's barroom right away. The company manager had a fearsome temper and the driver didn't want to do anything to provoke it, so instead of quenching his thirst immediately as he would have liked, he gave his attention to his given task. Finally, when his wagon was loaded with supplies, he allowed himself a stop at the local hotel, where he spent a few hours drinking with friends he hadn't seen for a long time.

Caught up with socializing, the driver lingered too long and the sun was already setting by the time he excused himself from his drinking companions. He cursed himself for his stupidity; if he wasn't back by morning the company manager would notice his absence and tear a strip off him. He'd be lucky if he wasn't fired on the spot. Unwilling to face such dire consequences, the driver decided he'd leave now and push on through the night, despite the danger of navigating the rugged road blind. Slightly inebriated, he climbed onto his wagon and urged his horses forward down the darkening road toward Kidd's Landing and a warm bed. A bottle of whisky was tucked up against him on the bench, which he eagerly nipped at as he urged the team on. The heavily laden wagon rattled down the dirt track, and with each passing mile the sun dipped farther beyond the horizon, casting the forest into shadow.

By the time the wagon reached the crossing over the Pickerel River above Dollar's Dam, the night was pitch black and the driver was completely drunk. At the approach of the long wooden bridge, the horses suddenly froze in their tracks and refused to cross. The driver snapped the reins in irritation, but the horses remained stubborn, sensing some unseen danger ahead. By now angry, the driver cracked a whip over their backs, and only then, startled by the stinging pain, did the horses finally move forward onto the bridge. In the darkness and with his mind clouded by alcohol, the driver didn't notice that a flood had carried away the middle section of the bridge. He cracked his whip and snapped the reins, urging the hesitant horses onward and directly into the looming gap. The horses and wagon fell into the swirling waters below, taking the terrified driver with them.

His body was never found, so he was never given a proper burial. Perhaps that's why the spirit of the man revisits the scene of his demise, supposedly most often on nights of a full moon. His ghost urges his horses through the night, still trying to complete the journey to the logging camp he never got to while on the earthly realm.

According to John McFie in his book *Now and Then: Footnotes to Parry Sound History*, a man named Bain used to regularly share his encounter with the Wild Wagon as a fireside story. McFie recounts it this way: "One night on the Thirty Mile Road, when he [Bain] stopped to rest his horses, he heard another team and wagon approaching at a headlong pace. Bain pulled off to the side to give the careening rig right-of-way, and waited for it to pass. And waited. It kept coming, and coming, but never came."

Others have had similar experiences in the woods around Dollar's Lake. A woman was hiking along a trail one fall day when a distinct rumbling and squeaking sound caught her attention. She looked up and saw nothing. She was puzzled because now, in addition to the rumbling and squeaking, she could also make out the rattle of harnesses, the pounding of hooves on wet leaves and the neighing of horses. She looked around; with the trees bare of leaves, she could see deep into the forest and yet found no source of the mysterious sounds. Scared out of her wits, the woman ran. Did this woman hear the road as it once was, during its busy heyday, possibly on that tragic day more than a century ago when the drunken wagoneer and his horses were swept away by the river and into folklore?

It seems the ghostly wagon is most active in autumn when days grow shorter and shadows stretch longer. It was during

October a few years back that a group of hunters found themselves in the crimson-coloured woods around Port Loring.
The men, each one a burly, no-nonsense kind of individual,
had spent the day stalking deer and the evening sharing tall
tales and a few beers. Then, one by one, they crawled into
sleeping bags around a roaring fire and fell asleep. Tomas had
been the last to doze off, tossing and turning for what seemed
like an eternity on the hard ground. Hours after he had finally
dropped off to sleep he awakened with a start. The fire was
a bed of glowing red coals with only a few tendrils of flame
dancing above. The other men were sound asleep. Nothing
stirred and he lay motionless for a few minutes, enjoying the
stillness of the night and the red glow of the coals.

The stillness was suddenly interrupted. Tomas heard
a sound: the soft scuffling of leaves and the rattle of wheels.
He sat up, fully alert now. The firelight flickered on the tree
trunks and stretched weird, dancing shadows across the landscape. The sounds of hooves and wagon wheels were closer
now and growing closer still. Tomas' mouth went dry. He
knew what he was hearing was impossible—no wagon could
pass through the dense woods, and surely no one would
attempt to drive one into the forest in the middle of the
night—yet the sounds were so distinct that he was certain he
was in fact hearing them. He listened for long moments as
the wagon slowly approached, the rattling and creaking
growing louder with each beat of his racing heart. The wagon
drew so near that Tomas could even hear the laboured
breathing of the horses and the flick of their manes, but he
still could see nothing.

Then a heavily laden wagon that glowed with the pale blue
light of the moon rattled into view. It passed through the

shadows and between the trees, so the now-quivering hunter never got more than fleeting glimpses, but he distinctly remembers the dead eyes of the man hunched over the seat, snapping invisible reins. The wagon passed by Tomas, no more than 25 metres away, then slowly receded into the forest. When it was gone, Tomas was rooted to his spot and shaking all over. In some ways it felt like he had just emerged from a dream. When he was able, he woke his friends and excitedly told them what he had seen. Predictably, they laughed him off. How could they believe him? Tomas barely believed himself. He never mentioned the matter again, not until he shared the story with us.

Many ghosts are restless spirits bent upon completing some task left unfinished in life. They are bound to our world out of a stubborn commitment to this task, reliving it endlessly until their goal is fulfilled and they can be at peace. Such is the case with the Wild Wagon of Parry Sound. The driver's last journey is replayed again and again in the northern woods. His ghost urges his horses through the dark night, desperate to complete his ride, heedless of the fact that the road he travels has long since been reclaimed by the forest and that the camp he seeks has been abandoned for more than a century.

The ghost wagon can never complete its final journey, and therefore is doomed to repeat it for all eternity. The tragedy is that the driver's recklessness not only doomed his own spirit to a tormented afterlife, but also doomed those of his faithful horses.

Ghosts of Cooper's Falls

It's amazing how when people hear the term "ghost town," they immediately imagine an abandoned village where the decrepit buildings are haunted by spirits of long-dead residents unwilling to leave their homes and businesses. They imagine that undead eyes peer out from behind boarded-up windows, and that as they climb rickety stairs toward a sagging front porch they are moving one step closer to an encounter with the paranormal.

We encountered this common misconception all too frequently while researching *Ghost Towns of Muskoka*, a book that was not about haunted communities but rather about communities that had fallen on hard times and as a result have all but disappeared. In other words, they were a ghost—or a mere shadow—of their former vibrancy. And yet, in at least one case, we discovered the common perception was not far from the truth.

Cooper's Falls is today a virtual ghost town. The general store has long since closed, the township hall across the road is weathered grey and boarded up tight, and alongside the road, partially obscured by an encroaching cloak of foliage, lie decaying cabins that were once home to early settlers. An air of morbidity hangs heavily over the town. It is a hush that instantly tells visitors that Cooper's Falls belongs more in the past than in the present. Some residents, no longer of the mortal world, similarly belong to an age long gone. The two hotspots identified for their ghostly activity are the two most beautiful and peaceful locations in the faded community: St. George's Anglican Church and the waterfall after which Cooper's Falls was named.

St. George's Anglican Church

Although only a small village even in its heyday a century ago, Cooper's Falls nonetheless boasted two churches, built side by side about a mile and a quarter west of the community. Both still stand today, reminders of past glory. It's been said that the spirit of Cooper's Falls rests within the oldest of the two sacred buildings, St. George's Anglican Church. Some people who are sensitive to such things suggest that the church is blessed with the spiritual presence of the village founders interred in the cemetery.

"A surprising number of people, including a couple of priests, have felt that the church was somehow special the first time they entered it to worship or conduct a service," says a former church warden, Len Glowa. "You can almost feel the presence of those who came before us in the wonderful old church." Here, worshippers get close not only to the Holy Spirit but also to the spirits of villagers of long ago.

St. George's Anglican Church has its roots in the earliest days of the village. Thomas and Emma Cooper, who established their homestead in 1864 and prospered despite hardship and struggles, were tireless supporters of the Church of England. It was in no small part owing to their religious enthusiasm—and that of their children who followed them—that the Anglican faith developed deep roots within the community. Thomas and Emma were certain it was only their faith that allowed them to survive their first few years on the wilderness homestead, isolated from civilization, surrounded by packs of hungry wolves that forced them to fortify their cabin upon nightfall, struggling to plant crops in thin soil, and often living on the verge of starvation. The fact that

A ghostly congregation attends St. George's Anglican Church.

Thomas and Emma survived and eventually prospered, they were certain, was a gift from God, and they meant to repay it.

By 1874, other settlers had arrived in the area and Thomas and Emma established a congregation that would meet in the local schoolhouse. Later, they were instrumental in having a real house of worship built. St. George's Anglican Church officially opened on Sunday, October 26, 1884.

The church was also a reminder of the fleeting nature of human existence. One of the most distinctive features was a stained glass memorial window dedicated to William C. Cooper, who died in 1924 after being fatally injured while working in his sawmill. He left a widow and nine young children. William's passing marked the end of a rough few years for the Cooper family; Thomas had died in 1918, and his beloved Emma had joined him in 1923.

Coincidence or not, it was around the time that the village founders died that Cooper's Falls began the slide that saw it eventually reduced to a ghost town. The loss of the local logging industry and the strain of farming in the harsh northern climate proved too much for most of the villagers. One by one, families moved away in search of greener pastures and buildings were boarded up behind them. As neighbours left and village landmarks began to disappear, those troubled locals who remained behind sought comfort in the church. St. George's was one of the few constants in Cooper's Falls, seemingly immune to the trends that worked against the community. Desperately clinging to something tangible of their past, something to retain their communal identity, residents fought to ensure that their church survived.

Sadly, it seems as though their fight has ended in defeat. A few years back, the archdiocese decided that the church was to be deconsecrated and closed, perhaps even torn down. The announcement occasioned an outpouring of grief and even anger. Len Glowa was particularly hard hit by the decision. He found himself wondering what the reaction of those buried in the cemetery would have been to the news that the church was being closed, possibly even demolished. After all, the defining events in these people's lives—birth, marriage and eventual death—were celebrated within that building. Based upon the number of spectral encounters that have surfaced in the past few years, it's probable that the spirits of the dead have grown restless with the turn of events.

Len Glowa had an experience a few years ago that opened his eyes to the possibility that St. George's Church has a spectral congregation. While walking by the church one Sunday afternoon, he noticed a vehicle parked on the side of the road. Having lived in the town for as long as he had, Glowa pretty much knew all the cars in the area, but this one he did not recognize. "I thought it could be someone simply visiting the grave of a family member or friend, which is a common occurrence, so I didn't think too much of it," Glowa explains.

Continuing his walk, he made his way past the church and then headed for his home just east of Cooper's Falls. As Glowa was approaching Frank Cooper's old general store, the century-old mercantile that stands at the heart of the former community, he noticed the same vehicle once again. "A man and a woman emerged from the car," he recalls. "They paused and started to read a monument that explains the village's history, and then proceeded to walk up to the old store. I thought perhaps they were looking for Frank, who was there every day except Sunday back then. I spoke to them and mentioned that Frank would not be there that day."

The couple apparently was not looking for Frank Cooper at all and had no connection to him or to the village named for his family. They were from Richmond Hill and had simply decided to take a daytrip up to Muskoka to take in the countryside. They explained that they were just curious about the interesting old general store (which dates back to 1906 and is one of the best preserved buildings in the community), as well as the historic cemetery and the stories the grave markers tell.

After a few minutes of idle conversation, the woman happened to tell Glowa that she had sensed the presence of several "happy" spirits in the vicinity of the church. She began her story somewhat hesitantly, fearing that Glowa might think her strange, but she explained to him that she was sensitive to the spirit world and could tell that the church and its cemetery were haunted by a number of spirits. All of them, he was happy to hear, were contented in their surroundings. They chatted casually for a few minutes more and then Glowa continued his walk home. It was a short conversation, but it made him consider the future of these spirits should the church be closed or, worse, torn down.

Another visitor to the area decided to explore the graveyard of St. George's Anglican Church after learning of the building's sad fate. She found the headstones fascinating and spent hours wandering among them, learning the names and reading the often tragic ways in which the deceased met their demise. She would shake her head in sadness when she came to a particularly tragic story. When she couldn't make out the names on stones that had been aged smooth by years of exposure to the elements, she would simply run her fingers over the cold stone, tracing what was left of the letters and numbers, "feeling" the stories of those who are at eternal sleep in the soil below.

Eventually, the woman found herself standing before the headstone of an infant who died a century ago and became strangely moved by the silent grey stone. "I could feel the sadness of the mother who stood at this very spot over 100 years ago," recalls the cemetery's visitor.

Perhaps the woman was connecting with the spirit of a still-grieving mother. After all, the loss of a child creates an overpowering sadness in any woman. It's a painful loss that time cannot erase, so painful that a mother may carry the heart-rending turmoil to the grave and beyond. Decades, even a century of mourning may not ease her suffering.

Suddenly overcome by a lingering chill that she couldn't explain, the woman left Cooper's Falls and returned to her friends' Gravenhurst home. Uncontrollable shakes continued well into the night and caused her to lie restlessly on the couch that was her bed. An extra sweater, thick socks, a warm blanket…nothing seemed to warm her up. It was as if someone with a cold hand had reached into her very soul and gripped her heart with icy fingers.

Just when she was about to close her eyes and try to get some sleep, she looked across the room and saw the antique rocking chair sitting in the corner start to slowly rock back and forth all on its own. Then all of a sudden she heard the faint sound of a baby crying. The soft wailing was clearly coming from the corner where the chair gently rocked of its own accord. Afraid at first, not knowing what to make of the situation, the woman soon felt an overwhelming sadness. She felt numb and almost dead, and yet she found herself wiping tears from her eyes.

The emotions from her spiritual connection were so real and so consuming that she quickly became totally drained. She drifted off into a deep sleep, but with sleep dreams can come, and they did for her. The dream that visited her that night was particularly vivid. "I was in a bedroom of a decaying home. The bed had ripped and tattered sheets that had seen better years. The smell was of must and mildew, and the floorboards were creaking and sagging," she recalls of her dream. "Most importantly, there was a rocking chair by the window, stained and covered in dust."

Was this woman somehow connecting with the building that the dead child once called home, as it would appear in its decaying state today, or was it simply a fantastic dream? We can't say for sure, but what is certain is that the memory of St. George's Anglican Cemetery will haunt this woman for years to come. To this day she regrets not driving the back roads around Cooper's Falls to see whether there was an abandoned and weathered home that matched the one in her dream.

Many people who pass through Cooper's Falls might simply see a ghost town strewn with relics of days gone by—relics in the form of a general store with a rusted gas pump out front, twin churches surrounded by rows of headstones, numerous weathered and decaying buildings. But for others who care enough to stop and listen, the village is still alive, and they can hear the stories told by the souls who lived and died here.

As for the fate of St. George's Anglican Church, at the time of writing it remains very much up in the air. "What would happen to the ghosts that frequent the area of the church if it were moved or demolished?" Len Glowa wonders thoughtfully. "Let's hope that they are not disturbed."

The Falls

Amidst all the decay and sadness that seem to envelop Cooper's Falls, there is one beautiful thing remaining: the waterfall for which the community was named. But even here, with beauty there is tragedy, and where there is tragedy there is often a lingering ghost.

The spirit of William Cooper is ever-present at Cooper's Falls.

Waterfalls were very important to the residents of any nearby community. They provided power to operate mills, which provided vital services, such as grinding grain for flour or cutting lumber, and also offered jobs to the people of the community. William Cooper, Thomas' son, built a sawmill along Cooper's Falls in 1921 and ran it successfully for four years; then operations came to a sudden and tragic end. One day in 1925, William had a horrible accident at the mill and was severely cut up by the machinery. He needed medical help fast, but the roads were impassible. It was early spring and the snow was just beginning to melt away, transforming the primitive roads into something like a stretch of quicksand in which cars or buggies would sink up to the axles and become hopelessly bound.

Still, the people at the mill that day tried as hard as they could to help William, who was in agonizing pain and slipping in and out of consciousness as he lost blood. They took him by boat to Washago and then by train to the hospital, but they arrived too late; William had succumbed to his injuries. His death rocked the tightly knit community, and shortly afterward a stained glass window in his memory was installed in the church by his grieving family and neighbours. The death of William also marked the death of milling in Cooper's Falls; no one stepped forward to run the sawmill ever again.

But even though the mill has been gone for over 80 years, people who visit the area have on occasion heard the whining sounds of the saws over the roar of the river, a ghostly record of the sawmill's brief period of operation and the tragic death that occurred there during that time. In addition, photographs of the waterfall and its surroundings have been known to reveal unnatural glowing orbs—moisture, or spirits caught on film?

On a bright midsummer's day in 2007, a couple visiting the area eagerly made the walk to the waterfall, excited to see this natural spectacle that had played such an important part in the village's development. As Richard and Teresa walked the narrow path to the water's edge, Teresa began to feel like she was being watched. She looked around, searching the woods, but other than Richard, there was no one in sight. She didn't feel scared at all; it was odd but hardly unusual for Teresa to have such sensations. Sensitive to the spirit world, she was accustomed to having these sorts of feelings every now and then when exploring history, as she and Richard were so fond of doing. Whether she was connecting with the spirit of a playful child in a cabin lost in the woods or being overwhelmed by the violence of a War of 1812 battlefield, it seemed like the past was always ready to greet her during their adventures.

Teresa put aside the sensation of being watched and tried to focus on the enjoyment of the moment. She took pleasure in the warm sun and the invigorating walk through the rich, green forest. Soon, the pair was overlooking the Black River. Neither one spoke as they soaked in the view of the thundering falls. It was here that Teresa began to feel a strong, manly presence nearby, but it wasn't her friend. Instead, it was an otherworldly presence, that of a spirit who she instinctively felt was trying to keep her away from the riverbank so as to prevent her from falling into the water.

Even when she dared to climb down the steep bank and walk from rock to rock along the river, trying to get to the bottom of the falls to capture a close-up photo or two, she refused Richard's offer of a steadying arm. There was no need of assistance. Although her footing was unsure and the terrain rugged, she felt confident. She was feeling the chilled hand of another man, unseen but at her side, strong and reassuring, and she knew she was safe.

After taking all the pictures she wanted, Teresa made the climb back up the uneven rocks from the water's edge, once again feeling the cold hand assisting her. Back atop the bluff and safely away from the water, she no longer felt the ghost's protective grip on her arm, but she still felt his presence around her. In fact, the spirit followed her the entire way back along the trail to the road, and it was only when the couple reached their car that she could no longer feel him by her side. Many of us would be unnerved at the prospect of being accompanied so closely by someone unseen and unfamiliar, but not Teresa. Instead, she felt protected and secure.

Did this sensitive woman feel the presence of William Cooper, carefully protecting her while she made her journey to the base of the waterfall? She believed she did. In her mind, William believed one lost life at the waterfall was one to many. After all, waterfalls are to be enjoyed for their enchantment, not feared or connected to tragedy and horror.

Cooper's Falls is a ghost town in the most literal sense, a former village where spectral residents may well outnumber the living. Stories passed on to us suggest that one ghost remains tied to the thunder of the waterfall and several others to the peaceful sanctity of the cemetery. Who knows how many other spirits exist in the decaying cabins and abandoned farmsteads in the area? They probably see the village as it once was: a vibrant community, home to dear family and friends, where the future seemed bright instead of the sad, faded state in which it finds itself today. And so why leave?

Alsace Haunted Barn

The Alsace Road, south of Lake Nipissing and running between the villages of Commanda and Storje, is dotted with withered pioneer-era hamlets and the decaying remains of abandoned farmsteads. It's a road of broken dreams and lost hope, where the indomitable pioneer spirit was defeated and countless settlers lost years of their lives in a fruitless attempt to create thriving farms in the harshness of Northern Ontario. One can imagine bitter and broken spirits lingering in any number of the ruined buildings seen from the windows of passing cars.

This story focuses on just one of these tragic locations, a haunted barn partially obscured by a shroud of shrubs and trees and set amidst overgrown fields. At one time, this sagging structure was central to the ambitions of the farmer who built it. Valuable tools would have hung on its walls like trophies, crops painstakingly grown over the course of the year would have been stored in the loft, and livestock would have had shelter from the elements and predators inside its stalls. The barn had been a source of pride for the farmer, but now a dark horror holds court within its empty shell and rotting walls.

Early one October day, when the morning dew still glistened on the grass and the sun was just rising above the brilliantly coloured forest, a gentleman found himself driving along the old Alsace road. The road is mostly gravelled, so he kept the car at a low speed, wary of damage from pot holes or kicked-up rocks. In truth, he was enjoying the drive. The area was only sparsely populated, and there was a tranquility that the man enjoyed and seldom found. Rounding a lazy curve,

A nightmarish monster lurks within an old barn along Alsace Road.

he came upon a sagging barn with walls nearly consumed by vines and surrounded by tangled, overgrown farm fields. It was a scene filled with sadness, a farm that had failed to live up to the dreams and aspirations of its owners. The man pushed his foot down on the brake and slowed the car, allowing him to linger on the image.

Judging from the heavy lean of the building and the rotting wood siding, the barn had been abandoned for a long time, probably many decades. The driver had the inexplicable urge to peak inside it. Something called out to him, compelling him to pull the car onto the sandy shoulder and leave its warmth behind, push through a dense mass of wet, knee-high grass and weeds and then peak behind the barn's weathered doors. It seemed exciting, somehow, an adventure in an otherwise mundane life.

A few minutes later, the car was behind him and he stood in the shadow of the barn. Large spider webs covered the doorway, and the double-doors hung limply on their hinges. Driven by the thrill of discovery, the man brushed aside the webbing, heaved open the barn door and stepped into the gloom.

Immediately, he was struck by an overwhelming, musty stench of animals and damp straw that almost brought him to the point of nausea. "This doesn't make any sense," the man said to himself as his eyes slowly adjusted to dimness of the barn. "There's no straw in here, only broken farming equipment, and the barn obviously hasn't been used to house animals in many, many years. Weird."

He ventured farther into the barn, carefully stepping over rusting machinery, his boots crunching on rusty nails, aging beams groaning underfoot. Because it was so dark inside the barn and his vision still hadn't completely compensated, he moved slowly and with great care. But there was another reason for his caution, a tingling sensation on the back of his neck that told him something was amiss. Although he saw nothing strange or threatening, he nonetheless felt that there was something more than tools and abandoned farm equipment in the barn with him.

He stopped mid-step, frozen in motion, having noticed a large, dark shape in the shadow that formed below the hayloft. He took a few fearful steps back when a coal-black horse came out of the darkness toward him. It wasn't an ordinary horse, though. It had a scaly tail, like that of some sort of reptile, which whipped back and forth with agitation. It was also the largest horse the man had ever seen. It looked down on him with eyes, set into a massive head, that had the dull red glow of hot coals. With an evil whinny that sounded more like a wolf's snarl, the horse trotted forward.

The startled witness was sure it meant to trample him to the ground. Overcome with fear, he raced back frantically but just inside the door tripped over a floorboard and went sprawling. With the hellish horse almost upon him, he jumped to his feet and, ignoring the stinging pain in the knee he had landed on, ran headlong for the safety of his car. There were no sounds behind him—no hooves trampling the ground, no heavy breathing, nothing. The only sound was the beating of his heart, which rang in his ears like a hammer striking an anvil. But he could feel the beast's presence, its eyes boring into his back, glaring its hatred of all things living. His shaking hands were fiddling with his car keys when, with a suddenness that caused him to jump with terror, the silence was broken by a horrifying neighing that came from right behind him. He could feel hot breath on the back of his neck.

He wrenched open the car door and jumped in, locking up behind him. The man was shaking uncontrollably, his mouth dry with fear. He willed his eyes to look back toward the barn. He needed to be sure he was safe. To his surprise, there was no demonic black horse anywhere to be seen. He was sure it had been right behind him, a few feet away from trampling him beneath brimstone hooves, but now there was nothing. It was as if the horse had been swallowed up by the ground, perhaps being pulled back into the hellish regions from which it came. Moments later, the car was racing down the road and the ruined barn receding in the rearview mirror. But if the gentleman thought putting miles between him and the barn would distance him from the horror he had experienced, he was sadly mistaken.

In the weeks that followed, he began to have nightmares so vivid that he awoke screaming and dripping with sweat.

Most often the details of the dreams vanished as soon as his eyes flew open, but occasionally he remembered snippets that usually involved the midnight black horse with the hellfire eyes he had encountered in the barn. Worse, the terrors didn't always subside upon waking. Sometimes when he awoke in the middle of the night, he was certain he felt an evil presence in his room, watching him like a predator, almost feeding off his terror. The sensation always lingered for hours, preventing him from returning to sleep. The experiences got so bad that he actually feared going to bed at night. Only after several weeks passed and he had been reduced to a virtual zombie from lack of sleep did the incidents subside.

The gentleman in this story might simply have encountered a spectral horse, the ghost of a mare that has somehow been tainted by evil and driven to madness. But perhaps the creature he encountered was far more fiendish, a spirit with ancient roots that torments the living and causes terrifying dreams. After all, the word "nightmare" was originally the name of a demonic entity in the form of a pitch black horse with glowing red eyes that emerged from the darkness of night to cause bad dreams and claim human souls. Such spirits have been a part of religion and mythology throughout the ages, in Europe, Ancient Egypt, India and the Far East.

Regardless of exactly what it was he encountered, the man in this story may not be alone in experiencing it. When he began to ask around, searching for an explanation for what had happened, he came upon an elderly farmer who had lived his entire life in the region and offered a story that bore a striking resemblance to his own.

It was years ago, the farmer related in a hushed voice, in the midst of a particularly harsh winter. Snow storm after snow storm had battered the landscape, and weeks had passed without even a hint of the sun. When at last the skies cleared with the promise of a fine day, a farmer decided to take advantage of the break in weather to bundle himself up, grab his old rifle and go in search of a deer or rabbit to place on his dinner table. It had been a long time since he and his family had had fresh meat, and they were tired of canned beef and smoked ham.

Hours later, he was exhausted from snowshoeing through the soft, deep snow and was growing despondent because he had nothing to show for his efforts. Worse, he noticed that the sky had suddenly turned grey and angry, threatening more snow. He pressed on, figuring he had a few more hours before snow began to fall. He was wrong.

Blistering winds blasted through the skeletal forest, pounding the landscape without mercy. Then the snow began to fall like a shroud of white, reducing vision to the length of his arm. Battered by the winds and unable to see, the farmer had no choice but to seek refuge. He struggled onward, and with each passing minute he was filled with a growing sense of panic. If he didn't find shelter soon, he'd be in trouble. Just as his steps were faltering from weakness, he saw salvation in the form of the dark outline of a barn looming through the snow flakes.

The icy cold wind seemed to grow stronger now, as if trying to push the farmer back and keep him from reaching shelter. He summoned all his strength and trudged forward through the deep snow drifts, finally slipping through the barn door. Once inside, he collapsed on the ground, his strength spent. Hugging himself for warmth, he nestled into a pile of old straw. Hard as he tried, he could get no relief from the chill that gnawed at his bones. Even though he was now protected from the biting wind, he shivered uncontrollably. The cold of the merciless winter had been replaced by the unnatural, eerie chill of the undead.

Desperate to warm himself, the farmer tried to focus on what was around him. Perhaps there was something with which to start a fire, or an old tarp he could wrap himself in. His breath left him in a frightened shudder and he froze at the sight of a pair of red eyes glaring back at him from the darkened depths of the barn. His face twisted with horror as a coal black and yet vaguely transparent horse stepped forward from the darkness. Steam rose from snorting, flared nostrils and fiery eyes grew more intense as the creature came closer. This was no ordinary horse; it was something evil and sinister. There was a distinct air of menace about this animal that caused the farmer to run for dear life. He burst through the door and into the midst of the winter storm. The cold winds that pounded like a mallet didn't seem as bad as the dark entity inside that barn.

By this point in telling his tale the old farmer was pale, and his withered hands shook slightly. "The feller eventually made it home, but it was a near run thing. He darn nearly died out there and was so badly frost bit that he lost several fingers and toes." Grey eyebrows furrowed together in thought, his eyes faraway. The farmer ran a rough hand, missing a forefinger, over a face whose lines seemed to grow deeper as the story progressed, and the next words came out as little more than a whisper: "I'll be damned if I don't relive that day in my dreams even today." He was that farmer.

If you've ever half-woken from a terrible dream to find your body paralyzed with fear and a malevolent presence in the room, you too may have been visited by a nightmare. Even safe in your home and tucked snuggly in your bed, such experiences can be traumatic. You fear returning to sleep in case the horror revisits you, and you begin to see monsters lurking in every shadow. Just think then how horrifying it would be for such a nightmare to be reality, to come face-to-face with an evil spirit that is the embodiment of our worst fears. The fact that this spirit takes the form of a horse, an animal that has been closely associated with humans since the beginning of time, only makes the experience all the more terrible.

So remember this story if, one day, you happen to find yourself on a scenic rural road and come across an abandoned barn. You may be tempted to push open the sagging door and enter the building; derelict structures, after all, have an undeniable way of calling out to us. Your sense of adventure kicks in, a growing sense of excitement urges you on, and visions of what you may find inside cloud your judgment. But some things are best left unexplored, and some buildings best left undisturbed. You never know what horror might lurk within, and a horseshoe for luck may not be enough to save you.

Chancery Art Gallery

Jim Gally was so completely engrossed in the artistry and technique demonstrated in a piece of artwork hanging on the gallery wall that he failed to notice the woman behind him. The first he knew of her was the nagging feeling of being watched that tugged at his senses. He finally turned around, expecting to see a staff member or another art-loving customer. Instead, his eyes grew wide at the sight of a white, vaguely human-shaped blur in the corner of the room. Terrified, he dashed out of the gallery, the painting instantly forgotten. He has never returned.

Thankfully for business, such experiences at Bracebridge's Chancery Art Gallery are extremely rare. Most people who come in leave completely unaware of the building's long tradition of hauntings. But for the owners, it's an entirely different matter. Strange happenings occur so routinely that they've had no choice but to accept that they share their business and home with a spectral resident. It comes with the territory when owning one of the oldest and best-preserved buildings in Bracebridge.

Now an atmospheric and welcoming centre for fine arts, the two-storey brick building, located along a narrow cobblestone lane with an Old World feel, dates back to the 1880s when Bracebridge was only a few decades old. It is one of few structures along Main Street that was not destroyed by the fires that periodically consumed the heart of town during the Victorian era. At various points over the past 130 years, the structure has been home to a tobacconist shop, a book store, a bistro famed as far away as Toronto for its fine food, and a hair salon.

Purchased in 2003 by Paul Ivanoff and Lena Kolobow, the building has been lovingly restored to its Victorian appearance. Many of its original features have been retained; the modern drop ceiling was removed to expose the original embossed tin tiles underneath, the hardwood flooring has been retained, and efforts were made to preserve old masonry that contained traces of the building's story. Period furnishings, including 19th-century church pews, an antique rocking chair and a working piano that dates to the 1840s, have been brought in to reflect the era in which the building originated. It's clear from the moment you enter that the owners have great respect for the building and its history.

Both Paul and Lena are practicing psychologists and psychotherapists, well educated and serious minded, trained to find rational explanations to life's mysteries. And yet, both are convinced that the Chancery Art Gallery is haunted. A wealth of baffling experiences in the years they've been living in the historic building has left them with no doubt of it.

"The hauntings began long before we took over the building," Paul explains, recalling a decade of paranormal experiences. "There was a restaurant downstairs when we began renting rooms on the second floor. The staff of the restaurant believed there was a ghost here. They'd hear footsteps when there was no one around, as well as other strange, inexplicable noises. It wasn't long after we moved in that we began to believe as well. This building is most definitely haunted."

But their introduction to the paranormal took place many years earlier and half a world away. Both husband and wife were born and raised in Russia, and shortly after getting married they found themselves renting rooms in an old home in St. Petersburg, an ancient city that has seen more than its fair share of tragedy and disaster. Many paranormal researchers believe St. Petersburg to be heavily populated with ghosts.

"The home we moved into was more than 100 years old," began Lena as she fondly reflected back on the beginning of a happy life spent with her husband. "One day, I left my wedding ring sitting on an old antique table, and when I returned for it later the ring was gone. It had just disappeared. I couldn't find it anywhere. A few days later, both Paul and I looked at the table at the same time, and there it was. There was no explanation. Nobody could have come into this room, and we knew we had thoroughly searched the room for the ring when it first went missing. We spoke to the old lady who owned the home, and she said this sort of thing happened all the time, that items were always going missing and then would suddenly turn up. I was just glad to have my ring back, but it was very strange."

As a result of that puzzling experience, and others like it during their time living in that old home, the couple was not frightened when, many years later, they immigrated to Canada and moved into what is now the Chancery Art Gallery only to find that it also had a resident ghost. But nothing could prepare them for the variety of unsettling ways in which the spirit revealed its presence, and the frequency with which it did so. There were times when the paranormal activity even caused these highly educated doctors to question themselves and their grip on reality.

Lena was the first in the family to notice something amiss. "It began right after we moved in. I would wake up in the morning and find my bathroom towels wet, soaked, as if someone had just taken a shower. My toothbrush would also be wet, as if it too had been used," she explains. "This made no sense to me. Why would my husband or son use my towel or toothbrush? They wouldn't. And when I asked them about it, of course they both told me they hadn't used them. This would occur every day for about a week, always first thing in the morning, and always both the towel and the toothbrush. Then, suddenly, it would stop. A while later, maybe after a few weeks had passed, it would start up again. There is no explanation."

Beyond that, Paul and Lena found that the faucets would occasionally turn themselves on. They'd be downstairs in the gallery and hear water running in their apartment above. Racing upstairs, they'd find water pouring out of the bathroom taps. Not a slow drip, mind you, as would occur if someone had simply not turned off the water completely, but a steady stream of gushing water. Interestingly, they discovered that the exact same thing is reported in the Griffin Pub, an old building located across the lane where the spectral image of a woman is often seen.

Another frequent experience is phantom footsteps that walk across the aged floorboards. Oftentimes, Paul or Lena would be working in the basement when they would suddenly hear the distinct sound of someone walking on the floor above, in the gallery. They'd run up the stairs, assuming a customer was there waiting to be greeted and served, but would find no one. For a time they tried to tell themselves that it was the sound of the building settling, as old buildings tend to do, but they realized they were fooling themselves. The sounds were too distinct to be anything other than footsteps, and you could trace their movement across the floor. Slowly, they came to accept that what they were hearing was, in fact, a spirit wandering the premises.

Many buildings reputed to be haunted are plagued by temperature extremes, and the Chancery Art Gallery is no different. Sometimes, it suddenly and inexplicably grows very cold in certain localized spots within the gallery. One minute you're comfortable, the next you step into a pocket of teeth-chattering cold. Within seconds your fingers grow numb and your toes begin to curl in your shoes. Then you take a few steps and just as suddenly the chill fades. What precludes a normal, rational explanation is that these cold spots move at random, rather than being experienced in predictable locations. The bubbles of freezing temperatures develop routinely, at least once every other week, and have become so much a part of the building's quirks that Paul and Lena no longer run to check the thermostat every time one occurs.

The family cat is particularly sensitive to the spirit's presence, which is not at all surprising since there is much evidence to suggest that animals are more attuned to psychical influences. She will often stare at the walls, alert and unmoving, as if warily watching something that human senses can't detect. It's a different response than when she watches squirrels or birds outside the windows, when her tail twitches with curiosity and she purrs quietly. Instead, the cat seems rooted to the spot, completely unmoving as if frozen with fear, the fur on the back of her neck rising on end. Their pet is not otherwise skittish, but Paul and Lena witness this odd behaviour about once a week.

Many staff members and even some gallery customers report oddities. Shadows that shouldn't exist and which have no source are often seen. When the shadows move by themselves, creeping along the floor or extending up the wall, witnesses are understandably frightened. Mysterious footsteps are not the only unearthly sound heard; on one occasion a browsing customer heard a whispered voice that sounded as if it came from directly behind her, but when she spun around, she found she was completely alone. Many visitors report the hair on their arms standing up, as if their sixth sense is alerting them to the unseen presence.

"We have an older woman who works here in the summer, a really nice lady," Lena explains. "The first time she came in looking for a job, she knew instantly the building was haunted. She sensed it. Like us, she experiences the ghost often and gets scared sometimes. In particular, she doesn't like going into the basement alone."

Paul and Lena are convinced that the ghost lingering within the art gallery is that of a woman, and though she's shy enough to remain mostly unseen, Paul believes he saw her once. "I was in the office one day and saw Lena—or who I thought was Lena—pass through the gallery and go downstairs into the basement. I went down after her to speak with her, but I found the basement empty. There was no one down there. I was confused because there's no other way out of the basement except up that staircase and through the gallery, and I would have therefore seen her leave. I called upstairs to Lena and she answered from our apartment. She had never come down. I know what I saw; it was absolutely real, and it was absolutely a woman. I must have seen the ghost."

The couple instinctively knows that the ghost means them no harm, and they have accepted her as a part of their home and business, something ingrained in the building's aging brick and mortar that they took on when they signed the deed. But they also believe she is tragically lost and confined to a world to which she no longer truly belongs. Who is she, and what deep sadness keeps her from crossing over to the peace and tranquility of the afterlife?

It has been suggested that the ghost of the Chancery Art Gallery and that of the Griffin Pub are one and the same, that the restless spectral woman is not limited to a single building but rather tied to the vicinity of Chancery Lane. In light of the eerily similar experiences reported in both buildings—phantom footsteps, taps that inexplicably turn on by themselves, the appearance of a female apparition—it does seem likely that the two buildings share the same ghost. There is also speculation that this ghost is related to the evil entity said to stalk people along Chancery Lane, that the two spirits are bound together by a shared tragic story. If these assumptions are true, then a possible identity for the mournful woman lingering within the art gallery emerges, and we can begin to understand the turmoil that keeps her from resting even long after death claimed her mortal body.

In 1918, Andrew Solave and his wife, Lena, purchased a farm several miles northwest of the village of Melissa. Slovakian immigrants, they had spent many years in Toronto toiling on factory assembly lines, working long hours and barely making ends meet. Now in their middle years, they were looking for a peaceful piece of land to call their own and on which to spend the remainder of their lives. The farm they settled on was a typical bush lot, rustic, heavily wooded and far from civilization, but it was theirs. The quiet, hardworking couple threw themselves into clearing the land and cultivating crops.

Three years later, the Solaves had made marked improvements to their simple farm and were beginning to reap the reward of their tireless labour. They were content and well liked by their neighbours. Then, on the afternoon of December 13, 1921, with the sudden crack of pistol shots that echoed through the snow-stilled forest, their happiness was shattered. George Cyr, a young neighbour who had spent time in jail for previous offenses, came upon the Solave home and drew a pistol from the pocket of his heavy winter coat. In a hail of bullets, he gunned down Lena and Andrew, along with a neighbour, George Wethers, who happened to be at their home. Wethers was shot three times and died. Andrew, shot twice, managed to escape into the woods. Lena was killed by a single shot to her back as she attempted to flee.

Cyr's motivation for the rampage made the deaths of Lena Solave and George Wethers all the more tragic. Living in a ramshackle farm house, without a job or other means of income yet supporting a mother and sister, Cyr was always on the verge of destitution. He used fear and intimidation to make ends meet and took whatever he wanted from other settlers in the area. He had a hair-trigger temper and, when riled, was as unpredictable as a Texas tornado. But this backwoods thug was still only barely putting food on the table. What he needed was a big score, and he saw his opportunity when he got wind that the Solaves' son, who was away working on the railroad, had sent them a large sum of money to pay for their farm. With pistol in hand and murderous intent in his heart, he headed to his neighbours' farm to take the cash and eliminate anyone who could point the finger of blame his way. But Andrew Solave survived.

George Cyr was hanged for his heinous crimes, his body buried in an unmarked grave atop Chancery Lane. The murderer's malicious ghost is said to rise from his forgotten plot after dark and, slinking through the shadows, stalk people who foolishly enter the lane after sunset. He's a frightening spectre, one of the most dark-hearted in Cottage Country.

It's possible—some would argue probable—that Lena Solave is the female spirit encountered in both the Chancery Art Gallery and the nearby Griffin Pub. If anyone should be restless in death, it is Lena. Cyr took everything from her: he ended her life even as she pleaded for it; his bullets separated her from her beloved husband; and with his greed and spite he destroyed her dreams for a happy future. Perhaps Lena Solave willfully remains in our world to torment Cyr's soul, haunting him if you will, as a way of ensuring he cannot forget his vicious crime. Or maybe the two restless spirits are shackled together by powerful emotions emanating from the violence of December 13, 1921, murderer and victim, unwilling partners forever bound together by the events of that fateful day.

Lena Solave may well be offering hints that it is she who haunts the Chancery Art Gallery. We believe the ghost intentionally targets the towels and toothbrush belonging to another Lena, that these antics are her way of letting the building's current occupants know with whom they share their residence. The ghost's fixation with water may also be another clue to her identity, as the Solave farm was located alongside Lake Waseosa. In fact, Lena died within sight of it.

But regardless of who haunts the Chancery Art Gallery, its owners are happy for her company. "We respect her and want to live in peace with her," Paul says, pointing out several ways they've attempted to make the spirit feel welcomed. "Some of the things we experience here can be strange, but for us it is normal now."

Because of their background in psychology and the way in which the brain functions, Paul and Lena are able to discount phenomena with rational explanations. They are even cautious about believing close friends who report seeing weird shadows or hearing strange sounds while visiting them. After all, since many are aware of the ghostly happenings within the building, the power of suggestion may well influence their perceptions. Nevertheless, even discounting every experience that may have a plausible cause, there remains a deep pool of unexplainable phenomena that has led to a firm conviction that the Chancery Art Gallery is haunted.

Does either Paul or Lena find it difficult to reconcile their scientific training with their absolute belief that the art gallery is haunted? Not at all, in fact.

"If physical matter doesn't end but is simply recycled, then the same should apply for the spark of life and human consciousness," Paul explains. "Theoretically, ghosts are very possible. I do believe there is likely something after death.

"Just because we don't have a scientific method of explaining something doesn't mean it doesn't exist. In our case," continues Paul, "natural explanations are not enough to explain the things that are happening to us. By definition, they must be supernatural."

Georgian Bay Ghost Ship

Ghost ship. The very term conjures up nightmarish images of a spectral vessel emerging from a bank of fog, coalescing from the greyness like a menacing phantom. Sails hang tattered and lifeless, the mast creaks and groans and seaweed clings like oversized leeches to the rotting hull. No one moves about the deck and a silent blanket of morbidity hangs over it. The ship, sent to the lightless depths of the ocean floor years before, dragging with it the souls of passengers and crew alike, is now a lifeless shadow that serves as a dark reminder of the sinister power of the sea.

This imagery is common to stories from every country around the globe. In fact, the most legendary ghost of all is a spectral vessel, the *Flying Dutchman*. With the widespread popularity of such tales, it should come as no surprise that Georgian Bay has a ghost ship to call its own. In fact, if stories are true, it has several; after all, this body of water is one of the most notoriously unpredictable and violent in the world. Georgian Bay is a veritable graveyard, its depths having claimed dozens, likely even hundreds of ships over the past two centuries. The *C.C. Martin* was one such casualty, lost during a late-season voyage to Byng Inlet. It's believed that she sails the waters to this day, her wraith of a skipper vainly trying to bring her safely into port.

During the early 20th century, Byng Inlet, located at the mouth of the French River along the wild northern shore of Georgian Bay, was a vibrant sawmill town home to one of the largest mills anywhere in Canada. At the time, the community rivalled Parry Sound in size and wealth, and residents looked to the future with optimism. As long as there were

Looking much like the tug in this photo, the *C.C. Martin* rises from the depths to bring warning to anyone who sees her.

trees to be cut down in the densely forested interior—and every spring thousands upon thousands of logs were sent down the rivers to the awaiting mills—Byng Inlet was assured its prosperity.

Byng Inlet may have been a going concern, but it was hardly an attractive community. Its harbour was perpetually clogged with a floating mass of sawdust and countless logs, smoke and steam lingered in the air like fog, and rare was the day when the whine of saws could not be heard carrying through town. It was also isolated, with the waters of Georgian Bay being the only reliable means of transportation. Everything coming in or going out went by boat of one shape or another.

Delivering the cut lumber from Byng Inlet to ports farther south was the responsibility of a fleet of hard-working tugs, which laboured throughout the sailing season to tow heavy loads across the often tumultuous stretch of water. Sudden-forming storms and gale-like winds would often cut adrift the tug, resulting in the loss of thousands of logs. On occasion, the tugs themselves fell prey to the fury of Mother Nature.

Sunday, September 20, 1912, was an unremarkable day, calm and pleasant. Captain George Vent was optimistic that he could deliver his tug, the *C.C. Martin*, and the barge it towed, the *Albatross*, to Byng Inlet without incident. It might be the last such trip to pick up logs before autumn's wrath closed Lake Huron to all but the largest ships and the most indomitable skippers.

The voyage began uneventfully enough, with the vessels making good headway, but shortly after passing Parry Sound, the weather took an unexpected turn for the worse. Temperatures plummeted, rain began to fall and the water began to roil in anger. Captain Vent prudently sought shelter in Pointe au Baril for a time, hoping to wait out the worst of the weather.

After a few hours, however, Vent became impatient and decided to press onward, despite the misgivings of the *Albatross'* skipper, Captain Dean. Dean, an old salt with vast experience on the lake, saw danger looming in the angry sky and wind-tossed waters. He had aboard the barge his wife and four passengers, and he wasn't eager to gamble with their lives. But Vent was insistent, and nothing Dean could say would dissuade him from his reckless decision. As a result, the tug with its barge in tow pulled out of the sheltered inlet and back into the open waters of Georgian Bay.

By nightfall, Vent must have regretted not heeding Dean's warning. Sheets of rain pounded the tug's deck, washing across the planks and pouring over the sides. The hull seemed to groan in protest as the tug was tossed about the metres-high waves. Lightning flashed and thunder roared overhead. Soon the unwieldy *Albatross* began taking on water, and as its holds filled it began to settle dangerously low in the water. Captain Dean blew the vessel's whistles in distress before he ordered everyone into the 16-foot skiff to escape the foundering craft.

The crew aboard the *C.C. Martin* apparently didn't hear the *Albatross'* distress calls. They couldn't have done anything to help anway, as they were locked in their own life and death battle. Man versus nature: man lost, and the *C.C. Martin* disappeared below the surface of Georgian Bay. Two weeks later, three bodies were found washed up on shore, and nearby was a ramshackle raft constructed of cabin and engine room doors. From this evidence, we are able to piece together the final moments of the doomed *C.C. Martin*.

Shortly after the *C.C. Martin* became separated from its barge, it must have become disabled or run aground on one of the countless rocky shoals lurking just beneath the waves. The tug was taking on water at an alarming rate that quickly outstripped the pump's capacity to cope. Panicked, captain and crew realized the vessel was slowly sinking. Worse, they discovered that the lifeboat must have somehow broken free and been swept away into the night, forcing the crew to then hastily build the impromptu raft upon which they gambled their lives.

As the men floated away from their ship, they watched it sink out of sight. It was a moment of extreme loneliness. Darkness enveloped them, and bitter cold sapped their strength and their will. They clung desperately to the raft, but with each passing minute exhaustion gnawed further into their bones. Feeling isolated and abandoned, despair began to take hold. They slipped into elaborate thoughts of being reunited with loved ones, but each man knew in his heart that he would never see his family again. One by one the sailors, their strength exhausted, released their grip on the raft and were carried away by lashing waves. None survived.

Ironically, the loss of the *C.C. Martin*'s lifeboat, a misfortune which ultimately cost the lives of all aboard the little tug, actually ended up saving the passengers and crew of the *Albatross*. Hours after the *C.C. Martin* slid beneath the waves, Captain Dean spotted its lifeboat floating aimlessly upon the white-capped waves and managed to pull alongside. And not a moment too soon, for his overloaded skiff was close to being swamped. Divine providence saved them; able to distribute their weight between two boats, the passengers and crew managed to safely row into Byng Inlet later that evening after 20 hours in open boats upon the angry, unforgiving waters of Georgian Bay.

The two vessels, the *Albatross* and the *C.C. Martin*, remain at the bottom of Georgian Bay, their exact locations unknown, committed to watery graves by the stubbornness of the tug's captain. And yet, it's said that the *C.C. Martin* does not rest easily beneath the waves, rising occasionally with its undead skipper at the helm. It is his punishment to sail on into a condemned eternity as penance for causing the deaths of the men entrusted to his care.

With such a terrible end to its career, it is not surprising that seeing the *C.C. Martin* is believed to be an ill omen, foreshadowing the onset of a terrible storm or bad luck. Wherever the wind takes it, the lifeless tug leaves sorrow and death in its tragic wake. Stories about the eerie derelict spread across Georgian Bay in the years after it sank, with sailors claiming to have seen the listing and decayed *C.C. Martin* floating nearby their own vessel—and then suddenly vanishing. Mariners are a superstitious lot who love to weave a tall tale, so some skeptics argue that the *C.C. Martin* lives on only in their fertile imaginations. But mariners are also a tight-knit fraternity who respect the waters upon which they depend for their livelihood and who honour the memories of those whose lives were claimed by these same waters. To fabricate a story that reduces a maritime tragedy to a plot device seems out of character, so we choose to give sightings of the *C.C. Martin* some credence.

One stands out. In the autumn of 1932 or '33, on a grey but otherwise unremarkable day, a small fishing boat pulled out of Parry Sound. Her worn and weathered appearance reflected the character of her skipper, a hardworking old fisherman who had spent a lifetime struggling to eke out a living on the water. He headed out into open waters and spent the better part of the day trolling nets through a lake that was once bountiful with fish. It was late afternoon when the blanket of grey clouds began to dispense a chilly drizzle. Nothing to concern himself with, the old salt was certain, and he continued about his business.

A short while later he happened to look up and scan the horizon. He spotted a decrepit-looking tug sailing off his stern. The boat listed noticeably to one side, its hull broken and decaying. The fisherman rapped his knuckles on the worn railing of his boat in uneasiness. There was something oddly unsettling about the tug. It had seemed to suddenly appear out of nowhere, and not a soul could be seen moving aboard. Minutes passed. Now the fisherman could see the well-worn name painted on the hull: it was the *C.C. Martin*.

He then noticed with horror that the colour of the water in the boat's wake had changed to blood red. Fear rose within the man as he watched the *C.C. Martin* keep pace with his boat. Then, inexplicably, the tug simply faded from view. It didn't sail off, it didn't sink beneath the water, it didn't disappear behind an island. It was just there one moment and gone the next.

The fisherman had no time to breathe a sigh of relief. What he saw next was worse than a phantom vessel, and it caused genuine fear to swell within his chest. Like an approaching veil of death, a black line of clouds appeared on the horizon and rolled in with a fury. Blistering winds and a mix of rain and snow pounded the boat without mercy. The fisherman turned his vessel toward shore and raced for the safety of a sheltered cove in which to last out the storm. Tossed around by white-capped waves, bombarded by the wind and the rain, water crashing over her bow and swamping the wheelhouse, the craft struggled to make headway. With each passing moment, the fisherman grew more concerned for his safety. He began to silently pray.

The rain fell with a vengeance, the hardest downpour the man had ever witnessed in his six decades upon these waters. Lightning flashed, a sudden blast of brightness against the gloom, and thunder crashed a half-second behind. In that split second of illumination, the man swore he could see the derelict tug off of his boat's bow, being tossed about by the angry waves and then suddenly swallowed by the darkness. He had no time to consider the fate of that vessel; all of his concentration was devoted to holding onto the furiously spinning wheel that provided the only meager control he had over his own plight.

Perhaps his silent prayers were answered. Despite the buffeting of the wind and rain and waves, the tiny fishing boat somehow managed to pull safely into a bay where the tree-lined shores served as a barrier against the worst of the storm. When the weather took a turn for the better, the fisherman bolted back to Parry Sound, certain that he had narrowly avoided joining Captain Vent in his watery grave. He was also certain that Lady Luck was going to turn her smile elsewhere—you couldn't have it forever, and the fisherman had survived more than his share of dangers during his years spent on Georgian Bay. That realization hastened his retirement a few short years later.

Who knows how many others have seen the ghost ship and not been as lucky as this man? How many unfortunate souls have been claimed by storm or mishap shortly after encountering the cursed tug? How many boats that have sunk in Georgian Bay since 1912 have done so after crossing paths with the spectral *C.C. Martin*? Sailors cringed at the thought of spotting this ill-fated vessel, certain that doing so meant they would share the same tragic fate as its drowned crew.

The tug went down almost a century ago, the victim of her captain's arrogance and impatience as much as the temperamental nature of Georgian Bay. That's the real tragedy of the story, the fact that the disaster could easily have been avoided. Captain Vent has the blood of his crewmen on his hands, and it prevents him from finding any peace in the afterlife. Who knows when the tug, crewed by this undead captain tortured by unrelenting self-guilt, might finally sail into the great beyond?

Ghosts of Muskoka Heritage Place

Muskoka Heritage Place is a recreated pioneer village in Huntsville that uses carefully restored buildings and authentic artifacts to demonstrate what the frontier of Ontario was like in the late 19th century. It is one of Cottage Country's premier tourist attractions, and there's a tranquility about the place that makes it easy to imagine stepping back in time. With all the requisite sights and sounds, you're transported to the year 1880. In the dim interior of a log home, a pioneer woman bakes fresh cookies while her friend bundles herbs plucked from the garden and ties them to the rafters for drying. Farther up the street, yet another homemaker spins wool into yarn, while within the smoky interior of the blacksmith shop, a skilled artisan pounds metal into shape on his forge. A horse-drawn wagon slowly rumbles down the dirt street, its driver waving neighbourly at the innkeeper who rests lazily in the shade of his porch, waiting for guests to arrive.

Muskoka Heritage Place is home to nearly two dozen historic buildings that have been relocated from across the Muskoka and Parry Sound districts, including a village general store and post office, the Milford Bay Wesley Methodist Church, a typical pioneer one-room schoolhouse, a working saw and shingle mill, a First Nations seasonal camp and several historic homes. There's even a working steam train that chugs along a few kilometres of track and disembarks passengers at a handsome train station.

Each building has a story to tell, a spirit all its own, the product of the successes and failures, happiness and heartache of the men and women who lived and worked within them. More than just homes and businesses, to the pioneers of Muskoka these buildings also represented hopes and dreams for new opportunities. In some cases, the original occupants literally left their souls behind when their bodies moved on, as guests to the museum are occasionally startled to discover.

It's possible that each of the buildings has some spectral energy clinging to period furnishings, lurking in the cracks between well-worn floorboards, staining century-old walls. Here we focus on the two that seem most alive with spiritual activity: the Spence Inn, a former coaching hotel, and the deceivingly inviting Hill House.

Hill House

It's a fine September day, with the warm, late-summer sun reminding you of the sunbathing and swimming of the previous months. Feeling the irresistible draw of spending an afternoon outdoors, you decided to visit the historical pioneer village at Muskoka Heritage Place. It was a good decision, because now you find yourself thoroughly enjoying the adventure back through time, exploring one heritage building after another and slowly but surely being swept up in a wave of nostalgia.

You round a corner and a charming old home comes into view: the Hill House, according to the visitor's map you hold in your hand. There's something comforting about this building, like grandma's house, warm and inviting. You can almost imagine fresh baking cooling on the window sill. As if it calls

Even in death, Reverend and Mrs. Hill continue to preside over their home.

out to you, your pace quickens. Pushing open the door, you step into a home rich in period detail. But as soon as you're inside, the inviting feeling escapes through the open doorway. Replacing it is an eerie, uncomfortable, cold feeling. You feel unwelcome; you feel watched; you feel afraid. Instinctively, you know that spirits lurk within the building's aged walls. They're not visible, but they're there all the same, and for some reason they don't want you here.

It doesn't make any sense, though. The Hill House certainly doesn't match the iconic picture of a haunted house. When we hear the term "haunted house," we instantly imagine something sinister and frightful. We envision dried leaves crunching underfoot as we cautiously approach a dilapidated ruin of a home under the light of a full moon. An unnaturally cold wind whistles through trees that are leafless and bent. The roof of the house sags, diseased-looking vines strangle the walls, and mysterious forms loom in windows. As we climb rickety steps our whole body tenses, and we jump in fright as small animal bones hanging from the eaves rattle together like a sinister wind chime. The front door swings open lazily, as if beckoning us to face the horrors that lurk inside.

That's the haunted house of Hollywood movies and popular culture. It's an image that looms large in our collective imagination, and it carries with it a powerful emotional impulse: fear, revulsion and sadness. The Hill House, on the other hand, is about as far from that picture as you're likely to find. A quaint, two-storey wooden structure tucked away at the back of the village at Muskoka Heritage Place, it's warm and inviting, with neatly painted green trim, a welcoming entrance and impeccably maintained grounds. But appearances can be deceiving, because though flashes of lightning do not reveal grinning gargoyles leering down from the eaves and wispy cobwebs do not drape from the ceilings, the former home of Reverend Robert Norton Hill is very much a haunted house.

Countless guests walk through its rooms every year, passing from the drawing room and dining room on the main floor to the three bedrooms upstairs, marvelling at the authentic furnishings and the care with which the building has been preserved. They peer through a window in time into the life of a Methodist minister and his wife, seeing firsthand how a middle-class family would have lived in the 1880s. All except for a select few guests are blissfully unaware that when the building was relocated from Hillside, along came the spirits of its former owners. The couple remains in residence to this day, unwilling to vacate their beloved home. Unseen, they await each guest that passes through the door.

Generally speaking, the Hills don't mind the intrusion of people wandering through their home, even when the guests don't have the common courtesy to say hello or to introduce themselves. They shrug their shoulders and carry on, knowing that before long the strangers will leave and the home will be theirs once again. There are times, however, when the spirits do take exception to the intrusion. At such times, they like to let it be known whose house it really is, and they do so in dramatic, even frightening ways. As a result, while to most visitors the Hill House is just one of many historic buildings in the recreated pioneer village, to the staff at Muskoka Heritage Place its reputation is decidedly more sinister. Indeed, after a series of spectral temper tantrums, many staff fear entering the building alone, and some refuse to go in at all.

Robert Norton Hill was a humorless man of the cloth, a Methodist preacher strict in his beliefs and unbending in his morals. He spent many years ministering in the town of Schomberg, tending tirelessly to the spiritual health of his congregation. In 1867, he heard about the Free Land Grants in Muskoka while attending a Methodist conference in Toronto and was intrigued by the promise of bountiful farms and boundless beauty. By this stage in his life Hill was growing restless, and no doubt the challenge of homesteading appealed to his sense of adventure. Here was a new frontier to conquer, and in this wild and inhospitable country there would surely be countless settlers eager for the comfort of faith. Following his heart, Hill resigned his ministry and headed for Muskoka, where he hoped to find peace and contentment in working the land.

After investigating several parcels, Hill selected land on Fairy Lake. But one night he dreamed of a spread of land jutting out into the water, with an island directly in front of it. The dream was so vivid that Hill was certain it was a vision of the land fate intended him to have. The very next morning he set out on further explorations, canoeing around several lakes in search of the landscape seen in his dream. Incredibly, along the unsettled shores of Peninsula Lake he discovered a location identical to the land he'd seen in his vision and knew it was meant for him. He quickly claimed the 700 acres of fine farmland in what is today Hillside, a village that bears his name and considers him its founding father.

Although Reverend Hill turned out to be an accomplished farmer, he couldn't turn his back on God and his duty as a priest. Before long, he was tending to all of north Muskoka, which required lengthy and exhausting journeys by foot, horseback and boat.

As a result of his selfless missionary work and the important duties he performed as a district judge, many people greatly respected Hill and held him in high esteem. Others had a different view. They would say he was quarrelsome and domineering and would spitefully carry a grudge for years; some neighbours even accused him of being stingy or miserly. Sinner or saint, everyone recognized that he was a strong personality who played an important role in the development of northern Muskoka. He died in 1895 while running for parliament, and a loving memorial was erected in his name in the Hillside Methodist Church. Almost a century later, Reverend Hill's home was moved to Muskoka Heritage Place to serve as an important exhibit in the recreated pioneer village.

Teri Souter is the manager of Muskoka Heritage Place. She admits that the overwhelming evidence from staff members, volunteers and park guests alike points to the existence of ghosts within the Hill House. "There was an entire year when nobody on staff would close the house alone," she says. "People heard footsteps upstairs when there was nobody else in the house; they came into bedrooms and saw the bed looking as though somebody had been sitting on it; and even if they didn't hear anything they often felt that they were being watched."

While visiting the museum, we spoke with a pair of costumed volunteers who shared their fear of the building. Both admitted that though the Hill House generally feels friendly and warm, there are times when a creepy essence clings to the walls like festering mould. It makes them uncomfortable. Intrigued, we pushed for more details about the ghost. "Ghosts, not ghost," one of the women corrected matter-of-factly. "There's more than one in that building. Both Reverend and Mrs. Hill haunt it, a couple in death as they were in life."

More interested than ever, we urged them to continue. Mrs. Hill seems confined to the second floor, leaving her husband to roam around the dining room and drawing room by himself. Many people have sensed the presence of a woman watching them from an upstairs window, and on occasion a momentary glimpse of an elderly lady can be seen tentatively looking out at an unfamiliar world.

The most memorable incident involving the spirit of Mrs. Hill occurred in the autumn of 2001 during a Halloween event geared toward youngsters. The village was alive with the sound of children's laughter as dozens of little ones raced from building to building, thrilled by the novel setting and the festive activities. Perhaps all the ruckus and youthful energy annoyed old Mrs. Hill because she soon began acting out in an uncharacteristically dramatic fashion.

A group of children entered the Hill House, followed closely by their adult guardians. While most of the kids remained downstairs, chattering happily, several others raced upstairs on little legs, with two women close on their heels to ensure they didn't get into any mischief. The women kept a watchful eye on the exploring kids but took the time to peer into the bedrooms and appreciate the history they represented. Both admitted that if not for the near-maddening noise of delighted children at play, the home would be calmingly serene.

While peeking into the master bedroom, an antique hairbrush sitting atop a dresser caught the eye of the women. It was beautiful and ornate, clearly a prized heirloom, but what got their attention was the way it rattled and shook even though everything else on the dresser remained perfectly still. Suddenly, to their astonishment, the hairbrush flew off the dresser and past their faces, landing six or seven feet away. Now frightened, they hurriedly gathered up the children and raced downstairs, where between nervous gasps for breath they shared their experience with Sara White, the collections manager for Muskoka Heritage Place, who happened to be working as a costumed interpreter in the Hill House that night.

"They were ashen-faced and wide-eyed, and clearly scared," Sara recalls. "The way they described it was as if someone had smacked the brush with her hand and sent it across the room. Maybe the woman of the house was annoyed that her privacy was being invaded."

Details of the evening's excitement eventually reached Teri Souter, who was taken aback. She remembered being told by a descendant that Mrs. Hill had had beautiful hair and even as an old woman would spend a lot of time caring for it. It seemed an uncanny coincidence. Since then it's become something of a tradition to greet Mrs. Hill in the morning and say good night to her at the end of the day. Even those who claim not to believe in the paranormal take time for this courtesy…just in case.

Although it was just that one time that Mrs. Hill performed poltergeist-like mischief, she frequently makes herself known in a more subtle way. Look carefully at the ornate wrought-iron bed in the master bedroom. Do you see something unusual? There's an indentation in the quilt, as if someone had been—or perhaps is still—sitting there, looking at the dresser where the brush rests. The women who make up the bed swear the indentation isn't there in the morning and that it forms by itself during the day, always in the same spot.

Reverend Hill is widely believed to be the more strongly sensed ghostly presence within the home, which would make sense in light of his imposing manner and strength of character in life. Many witnesses also say this spirit can be moody on occasion, just as accounts say the man was. People credit him and his mercurial moods for creating the eerie atmosphere that sometimes envelops the home. It's not that the spirit is malicious, but he does like to remind people that he's the man of the house and as such deserves some respect. When respect isn't forthcoming, or when Reverend Hill simply wants his privacy, he acts out in an attempt to drive people off.

There's a big wooden chair in the kitchen that seems to be a favourite of Reverend Hill's. People often sense a powerful otherworldly presence sitting in it, and on one occasion, a hot, muggy summer's day without even a hint of a breeze, the chair was reported to begin rocking back and forth all on its own. Those who touch the chair sometimes feel a shiver run up their spine. A gentleman visiting the museum once made the mistake of sitting in the chair. He was hot and tired from walking and wanted to take a load off his aching feet, but as soon as he settled in the chair he was overcome by an uncomfortable sensation. The man felt unwelcome and intuitively knew someone strongly objected to him sitting in the chair. He jumped to his feet and quickly left the building, wanting to put distance between himself and the riled spirit. Was the reverend angered by an uninvited guest making himself so casually at home?

Once, a staff member heard the front door of the home creaking open and then closed shut. Then heavy footsteps made their way toward the drawing room, where Hill would have conducted most of his business affairs. The footfalls were slow and loud, as if made by a large man who was either old or tired. When the footsteps reached the drawing room, they suddenly stopped. The sound was distinct and clear, but there was no one in sight. Confused, the staff member searched the entire building, but the Hill House was empty.

To our knowledge Reverend Hill has never appeared before startled visitors, but he did pose for a photo once. This incident took place years ago, when several dozen members of the extended Hill family converged on Muskoka Heritage Place for a family reunion. For many of them, it was their first time seeing the home in which their common ancestors had lived. Later in the day, before people began to filter away, everyone posed for a family portrait outside the Hill House. The photo was taken, people embraced and wished one another well, and the reunion ended.

But the mystery was just beginning. When the photo was developed some weeks later, a man no one could identify was in the picture, posing along with the rest of the assembled family members. One person asked another who asked another; no one knew who this distinguished gentleman was, and neither did anyone remember seeing him present at the reunion. He would have been hard to miss, with his thick, wiry beard and stark, black suit. Finally, after all logical explanations had been discarded, it slowly began to be accepted that the individual was actually an apparition. Someone had the idea to look through old family photos, and sure enough they found the mystery guest among them: the long-dead Reverend Hill himself.

Wherever you go, whichever town you visit, residents can point to a local home plagued by restless souls. It seems every community has a haunted house, and the pioneer village at Muskoka Heritage Place is no different. The charming Hill House may not fit the stereotype of the haunted house, but even the most pretty and unassuming of buildings can be haunted. Just ask Reverend Hill and his wife; they're always home. And whenever they make their presence known to those of us still living, whether they do so in subtle fashion or in a skin-crawling moment of fright, they remind us that the buildings we explore while visiting the museum were once the homes and businesses of real people who settled this hard land.

Spence Inn

During the 19th century, roadside inns were common-place, located every 12 to 15 miles, about as far as one could reasonably travel over the course of day in the horse-and-buggy era. No one was turned away. Here, in these establishments, people could find a brief respite from the fatigue that came from travelling along the primitive, rutted roads. Exhausted, they would settle in for the night and await the arrival of daylight to start their travels anew. But not every tired soul continued on their way. Inns and hotels are among the most haunted buildings we find, suggesting that spirits are often reluctant to leave the warm hospitality and continue their journey into the afterlife.

The Spence Inn, preserved within the pioneer village at Muskoka Heritage Place and serving as one of its most popular attractions, is one such haunted inn. Many people have stayed here over the years, and its old floorboards have seen countless feet come and go—perhaps more came than went. Even after being moved from its original location and transplanted to the grounds of the museum, some guest rooms remain permanently booked. There is no longer a register to record their names, so we have to piece together their identities from folklore, the pages of history and eyewitness accounts of their spectral activity.

The Spence Inn is easily the largest building within the confines of Muskoka Heritage Place. Its size, the wrap-around porch and the grandeur of its furnishings instantly tell you this was a building of importance. But what isn't immediately apparent to wide-eyed visitors is the fact that this building is among the more mysterious locations on site, and that contained

At least two ghosts haunt the Spence Inn.

within its grey walls are ghosts and whispered legends of foul
misdeeds. Most tourists pass through its bar, kitchen and
guest rooms without knowing anything of its unsavory history. But every once in a while the past and present collide,
and the result is terrifying.

On a chilly October day in 2008, a woman decided to visit
Muskoka Heritage Place before the historic buildings were
closed up for the season. She was no ordinary woman,
however, and her visit wasn't idle interest in the region's
pioneer past. This woman was something of a sensitive, someone in tune with spiritual energies, and after hearing about the
mysterious events that occur within the inn she was compelled
to see it—feel it—for herself.

She stood outside for a few moments, marvelling at the
building and reaching out with her senses. The Spence Inn
felt warm and inviting, just as a roadside hotel should be. But

inside was a different story. Upon entering the building an instant chill spread throughout her body, and she knew it wasn't from the cool, late-season weather. The numbing cold only seemed to grow stronger as she walked up the stairs, but rather than be repelled by the unnatural chill, she knew to follow it. She came to a room at the end of the hallway that was made up to represent a physician's practice. It was so perfectly recreated that it looked as though the doctor had just up and walked away, leaving all his belongings behind.

The woman was pulled farther into the room. She sensed a presence there, an unwelcoming entity that scared her. Her eyes were focused on the Victorian wheelchair that stood before her, and slowly the misty image of a young soldier sitting in the chair came into view. His eyes were filled with sadness and pain. The woman realized she was witnessing a scene from back in time, a time long before she was even born. To her right, sitting in a chair at his desk, was the doctor. Neither of the spirits seemed to notice the woman standing just inside the doorway.

"Help me," the young soldier, perhaps just returned from World War I, pleaded. "I can't take the pain anymore, doc." The doctor reached for a vial of medicine and a syringe. "I'll take care of everything, son. I'll get rid of the pain. You won't feel a thing. I promise." His words were reassuring, but there was a coldness in his eyes that said something far different. The woman was shocked by his callousness and horrified by the way the doctor approached his patient, syringe held like a dagger, more predator than healer. Panicked and unwilling to watch anymore, the woman willed herself out of the scene and back to the present. Shaking uncontrollably from the experience, she fled the building. But she could not escape the terrifying image. It haunts her still.

What sordid past does the Spence Inn hide?

The inn was built in 1878 by Levitt Simpson, a 54-year-old gentleman who had just recently stepped off the boat from his native England. With his wife, Ann, and four children in tow, he headed for the wilds of Parry Sound District and took up a new life as a hotelier in the hamlet of Spence. Sitting alongside the Nipissing Road (which ran from the village of Rosseau in Muskoka to Commanda on Lake Nipissing), the inn was intended to cater to road-weary travellers passing through, and because it was located roughly at the road's midway point, Simpson named the establishment the Halfway House.

Whether Simpson had any experience in running a hotel is unknown, but he ably built the Halfway House into one of the finest anywhere along the Nipissing Road. The Halfway House was a place where people could find refreshment, stabling for exhausted horses and a place to sleep for the night. One dollar bought you a bed, but not privacy; guests of the same sex would be accommodated together in large rooms. For 25 cents you could also get a bath, though this luxury was likely only enjoyed by affluent travellers.

At the time, Spence was a thriving little community, home to two stores, a blacksmith shop, two sawmills, a church, a school and about a dozen log houses. Most of the 50 or so inhabitants were farmers, but the soil was too thin to provide for anything beyond subsistence-level agriculture. They, and the village they founded, were sustained by logging and serving the needs of travellers passing along the Nipissing Road.

Simpson sold the Halfway House around 1890, and it was then owned and operated by Donald MacEachern. Unlike his predecessor, who on moral grounds refused to sell alcohol within his establishment, MacEachern had no qualms about serving the "devil-drink." In fact, the first thing he did upon taking possession was build a sizable addition to the dining room to serve as a bar. Farmers came to drown their sorrows, imagining in their drunken haze that their fields were bountiful instead of rock-riddled and bare; travellers washed away the dust of the road with a shot or two of whisky; and loggers congregated to enjoy a taste of civilization after weeks or months spent in the bush.

There was a practical reason that MacEachern elected to begin serving alcohol. At the time, the railway was being pushed north from Muskoka toward Callander on Lake Nipissing, and MacEachern would have realized that when completed, this line would cause traffic along the Nipissing Road—the very foundation of the inn's prosperity—to wither away. A new source of revenue was needed to offset the losses, and the sale of alcohol was the logical choice.

Sadly, it wasn't enough to save the hotel. The completion of the railway in 1896 did indeed cause road traffic to decline, but far more so than most people would have anticipated. This development, and the fact that most of the failing bush farms were hastily abandoned around that time, spelled doom for the Halfway House. The once-bustling business began to change hands every few years, and with each sale its value decreased. Finally, it closed for good in 1911 and was purchased for use as a home by Hamilton Brown, a local schoolteacher who retired and took up farming. From that point on, the building served as a private residence. William Thomas Doherty was the last resident, living contented in the former inn for almost three decades.

By the 1950s, Doherty had passed on and Spence was enveloped in a ghostly shroud. No more than one or two homes were lived in, and the hamlet had been reduced to a handful of weathered and leaning buildings, crumbling foundations and cellar holes. The owners of the former hotel simply abandoned it, walking away from the malaise that seemed to cover the entire area. Decades passed and the inn decayed. Sad and neglected, it was close to ruin when, in 1977, it was moved to Muskoka Heritage Place. Throughout 1978–79, the Halfway House was painstakingly and accurately restored so that it looks today much as it would have a century or more prior.

Today, the building is an evocative reminder of the Victorian era in Cottage Country, as costumed innkeepers guide visitors through the rooms and the realities of 19th-century hotels. Tourists may not know, however, that one or more former innkeepers and tenants must have been particularly fond of their business because their ghosts walk the worn floorboards, having followed the building from the northern hamlet it once called home.

One of the rooms in which unusual phenomena most frequently occur is located on the upper floor, a room furnished as a doctor's office. There's an old wheelchair, shelves lined with medicine bottles, a desk littered with 19th-century stethoscopes and other early tools of the trade, and textbooks on human anatomy and the latest in Victorian medical practices. This room reveals an important role played by early inns: that of an office for dentists, salesmen or, as in this case, travelling doctors. Instead of paying for the room, these professionals would often provide services to the innkeeper and his family. Doctors would, for example, offer free medical visits and medicine in exchange for room and board. In this manner, small rural communities would gain the benefit of essential services that they otherwise would have gone without.

This room, indeed the entire second floor, is marred by an unpleasant spiritual presence that lingers to this day. Like a deep stain, this dark taint—the product of foul deeds gone unpunished—can't be removed, no matter how many years pass and how much the building changes over time. It's so deeply ingrained in the very walls of the inn that it's an inseparable part of its soul now.

During our investigation of Muskoka Heritage Place, we met a costumed staff member with a personal account that hinted at spectral activity in the doctor's office. While waiting out a chilling October rain shower, we warmed our hands around a pot-bellied stove in a log home and listened intently as she shared her tale.

"This happened a couple years ago," she began, speaking matter-of-factly and without embellishment. "I was on the ground floor of the inn when I heard a loud bang from above, somewhere on the second floor. It sounded like something had fallen, so I ran up the stairs and began searching the rooms for the source of the noise. I eventually found it: a big picture in the doctor's room had fallen to the floor for no reason. There was no wind or vibration that could have knocked it loose, the hanger was still firmly set in the wall, and there was no one in the building who could have knocked it down as a prank. I couldn't figure it out; there was no explanation for it. I remember a dark feeling in the upstairs that day, and I didn't feel welcome there. Since then, others have experienced the same thing, and it's always the same picture."

Another time, a family from Madison, Wisconsin, was exploring the pioneer village during a week-long vacation to Muskoka. They stepped onto the inn's porch, swung open the screen door, entered the building and stepped back in time. The family then separated, wandering singly and in pairs. One of the children, a 14-year-old girl, climbed the stairs and began exploring the second floor, snapping pictures of the guest rooms.

While photographing one room, she happened to look into an antique silver-rimmed mirror. She was startled to see that it wasn't just the face of a freckled teenaged girl—her face—reflecting back. Peering over her shoulder was the image of a jaundiced and bent corpse of a man, his eyes yellowed and his skin speckled with age. The girl could instantly tell he was a proud but bitter man, and there was something intimidating about the way he loomed over her shoulder. Startled, she spun around to see who the angry old man standing behind her was. To her surprise, and to her relief, there was no one there. She was alone, her body shaking with terror. Suddenly faint-headed, she leaned against the wall with her eyes closed, chest heaving as breaths came harder. After long seconds trying to calm herself, the girl finally felt strong enough push off from the wall and, on still-unsteady legs, descend the staircase. She found her parents, and in a burst of tears told them what she had encountered. Realizing the day of sightseeing was at an end, the family left.

Chilling experiences in the inn are nothing new and certainly pre-date its relocation from Spence. The museum archives have a letter indicating people had been complaining of spectral activity in and around the building during its time as a private residence. "One of the last individuals who lived at the inn when it was a house reported hearing and seeing all manner of weird things, such as ghostly carriages arriving in front of the house during the night," says Sara White, collections manager for Muskoka Heritage Place. "I can only hazard a guess that the individual mentioned was Mrs. Cecil B. Fraser (née Olive Doherty), since there is a letter from her in the inn research book. She was born in the house in 1920 and was raised there."

No one knows for certain who the ghost, or ghosts, inhabiting the Spence Inn were in life, but there are stories—legends, really—that offer suggestions. The tales surrounding the inn have grown taller with the passing years, more colourful and likely more filled with flights of fancy, but somewhere within these stories likely exists an element of tragic truth.

One story suggests that the ghost is that of an evil doctor, an incompetent and uncaring travelling physician who left a path of misdeeds in his wake. This man was more charlatan than physician, selling fake medicine, offering patients false diagnoses, botching even relatively simple procedures such as delivering babies or setting bones, and offering baseless advice. He preyed upon his patients, abusing their trust and his position. Guilt causes the ghost of the doctor to return to the Spence Inn, the site of so many of his most grievous lies. He languishes here, the former hotel now a prison for his soul, the continued restlessness of his spirit punishment for years of malpractice. Certainly this story corroborates the scene witnessed by the sensitive woman who visited in October of 2008.

There is another, even more scandalous story surrounding the Spence Inn that might explain its long history of hauntings. According to legend and whispered innuendo, a vagabond arrived at the inn one day, exhausted from his wanderings, starving, his clothes little more than rags that hung from his painfully thin body. The man had a wild look about him: he was filthy, his beard was ragged and streaked with grey, his stringy hair hung about his bony shoulders and his eyes darted back and forth like a caged animal. And yet, despite his appearance, the innkeeper and his family took pity on him, seeing the man beneath the savage.

Days turned into weeks, and the vagabond remained at the inn. He did odd chores to pay for his room and board and slowly became an accepted part of the family. The innkeeper was so consumed with his work and the elusive prosperity that was his goal that he didn't see the budding attraction between his wife and the man he had welcomed into his home. Running the inn meant long hours away from his wife, who grew increasingly lonely and began to seek companionship in the company of the vagabond. She couldn't help but notice the warmth that ran through her veins whenever he glanced her way, or how her pulse began to race at the touch of his hand. Love blossomed, and though her head told her it was wrong, the innkeeper's wife followed her heart into the arms of this new man.

One day, the innkeeper disappeared without a trace. His wife, with a well-rehearsed tale and equally well-rehearsed tears, sobbed that he had up and left her and her children, simply abandoning them to their fate. She played the role of the abandoned wife to the hilt, appearing hurt and vulnerable for her neighbours. No one suspected that this poor woman was anything but what she appeared.

A few months later, the vagabond slid into the position of both innkeeper and family man. There may have been some whispers in town that the relationship developed too quickly by the standards of the day, but most friends and neighbours were just pleased to see that the woman would be taken care of and that her tears had given way to radiant smiles. She had been scorned, after all; didn't she deserve happiness?

Soon, no one paid any thought to the relationship. It looked as if the matter was closed. One or two years passed, and then one day someone approached the young daughter of the innkeeper, all freckles and pigtails, and inquired where her father was. It was an innocent question, asked by a patron looking for the proprietor, but the answer rocked the community. "There," the young girl said sweetly as she pointed to the ground.

Word of the shocking revelation spread, and people began to question just what had occurred behind the closed doors of the inn. Had the innkeeper abandoned his family as everyone was led to believe, or did he lie in a shallow grave right under their noses? They had to know the truth. The area innocently pinpointed by the girl was dug up and, sure enough, a rotting body was discovered.

Folklore doesn't tell us what befell the vagabond and his lover. Did they flee the scene of their brutal crime under the cover of darkness and live the rest of their lives together? Perhaps frontier justice prevailed and the two murderers were stretched from the end of ropes. We can't even say for certain how much of the story—if any at all—is real. The line between fact and fiction can be a hazy one, and it grows more elusive as the years pass. But if there is any truth to the tale, it's possible that the ghost lingering within the Spence Hotel is that of the slain innkeeper.

The Spence Inn was once a popular stop on long journeys. Perhaps it continues to be today, except the guests now filling its register are not weary stagecoach passengers but spirits on the journey into the afterlife.

Manitou Islands Curse

At first glance they are unimpressive, non-descript—a group of small islands, shrouded by forest and almost featureless, rising from the waters of Lake Nipissing. But there's more to the Manitou Islands than first meets the eye, much more. Home to paranormal phenomena for centuries, they may in fact be a place of the darkest evil, having been corrupted by the lingering effects of an act of unimaginable cruelty and malice. The popular cruise ship *Commanda* maintains a respectful distance as it sails past; wise readers will likely do the same should they ever be in the area.

In total, there are five islands in the chain: Great Manitou, Little Manitou, Calder Island, Newman Island and Rankin Island. All of the islands are small, the largest being only a few hectares in size, but originally they were much larger. They evolved into their current shape and size in 1904 when the Chaudiere Dams were built on the French River and water levels on Lake Nipissing rose by about two metres. The natives to the region, the Nipissing people, probably would have been happy had the Manitous been submerged entirely. They largely avoided the islands out of fear and superstition, believing them to be cursed and home to angry spirits and restless ghosts. In fact, the name Manitou is an aboriginal word that can be translated as "devil." How did the islands get such a chilling reputation and ominous name? To find an answer, we must go back hundreds of years into the dark recesses of history.

Well before Europeans ever set foot in Ontario, there lived a beautiful young Nipissing maiden, a teenager but already a woman. Some admiring men in her tribe said she was perhaps the most beautiful woman they had ever laid eyes on. Her face was pure elegance—high cheekbones, full lips that split into a heartwarming smile, lust-stirring green eyes and perfectly shaped eyebrows to accent them. Her hair was long and black, shining in the light, and she walked with the grace befitting the daughter of a prominent chief. Her beauty and social standing meant that this girl didn't have to worry about attracting a future husband. She had the pick of any young, eligible man among her people and was actively pursued by many. Her aging father was proud of his beloved daughter and was determined that she would marry well and bring further honour to her already greatly respected family.

The maiden wanted to please her father and encouraged the attention of several young men, but she never found one who made her heart flutter and her pulse race. That is, until she met a dashing Iroquois brave. He came to her village as part of a peace delegation, for the Iroquois and the Nipissing were at war, and in the amount of time it takes for eyes to meet the two fell deeply in love.

The girl knew what she felt would displease her father and dishonour her family. The Iroquois were a savage, war-like people who had been the hated enemy of the Nipissing for generations. She was raised on stories of their brutality and had heard how they had destroyed the Huron and Neutral peoples, burning their villages, slaughtering the men and taking the women and children as slaves. She had even witnessed something of their ferocity herself, watching as war parties and hunting expeditions had returned to the village bearing the bodies of men killed in Iroquois ambushes. Yet she couldn't help but give her heart to the Iroquois brave.

Because their two peoples were bitter enemies, they knew their feelings could not be revealed. With the naïveté of youth they held out hope that perhaps the peace delegation, which lingered among the Nipissing all summer conducting talks and negotiations, would end the hostilities and they could announce their intention to marry. But until such time they carried on a secret relationship, meeting briefly but passionately under the cover of darkness. The courtship between the two young lovers was brief but powerful. Within the span of a few short weeks their love became all-consuming, an emotional bond that could never be broken. They would allow nothing and no one to interfere with their dreams of spending their lives together as man and wife.

Eventually, the young woman's family began noticing how she slipped away into the woods in the evening. Growing suspicious, her father and several of her brothers decided to follow her one night. With ease born of countless hours hunting, the men crept silently and unseen through the woods, stalking the girl as they would a deer. They watched as she skipped happily along a game trail, noting with growing unease her gaiety. They had seen girls in love before and recognized it in her now.

The chief and his warrior sons gripped their weapons tightly. They asked themselves who she was going to meet, but deep down every one of them knew the answer. Although they hadn't wanted to admit it to themselves at the time, each one had caught the longing looks between the young lovers and the fleeting brush of hands as they passed one another. But knowing their daughter and sister was in love with the Iroquois youth and was having secret rendezvous him didn't prepare them to discover the two lovers wrapped in each other's arms.

The men were enraged and humiliated. The Iroquois were the enemy. How could their beloved daughter and sister fall for one of them? It was a grievous insult to the family, the tribe, the entire people. The men burst from the forest and pulled the shocked lovers apart. The Iroquois warrior fought back, struggling against the strong arms of his assailants, but there were too many to fend off and he was quickly overpowered. The chief had to literally drag his daughter away from the fight; she kicked and clawed at him, desperate to get free and stop the brutal beating of the man she loved. When she realized she could not break free from her father's iron grip, the maiden began to plead for her brothers to stop their brutal attack. The men ignored her tearful begging. It wasn't until the hated Iroquois was unconscious and splattered with his own blood that the chief commanded his sons to stop. He didn't want the young man dead. Not yet, not this way.

The chief vowed to avenge his family pride and punish his wayward daughter. No one dishonoured him, certainly not his daughter. He would teach her a lesson and end the affair all at once. The Iroquois brave was bound and dragged to the shores of nearby Lake Nipissing, where he was thrown into the bottom of a canoe. The chief and his sons, roughly guiding the sobbing girl, piled in after him. They then paddled out onto the dark waters of the lake, heading for a collection of barren and uninhabited islands: the Manitous.

Once ashore, the men set to work gathering firewood and placing it around the base of a tree. Terror filled the Iroquois youth's swollen and bruised eyes as the terrible truth dawned. He was to be burned alive. The girl realized it too, and she screamed and begged and cried for her father to show mercy.

But he was beyond mercy, and in an act of unparalleled cruelty, he intended for his daughter to watch the gruesome end to her affair. If that didn't teach her a lesson, his rage-filled mind reasoned, nothing would.

The fire was lit, and as the flames grew hotter and higher the screams of the Iroquois man grew louder. But soon the night grew still save for the sound of the crackling wood and the girl's desperate sobs. As she watched the fire envelop the lifeless corpse of her lover, the young woman crumpled to the ground, his name on her lips. Her spirit was shattered. The trauma of watching the man she loved die was too much to bear. The flames not only consumed her lover but also her will to live. She threw herself into the raging fire, dying at her man's side.

Ever since that day, the Nipissing people have given the islands a wide berth, believing that the lovers wander the shores as restless spirits. What's more, they believed that the agony of the tortured souls had twisted and corrupted the islands into a place of growing evil. Trees and other plant life began to grow stunted; birds that flew over the islands would drop dead from the sky for no reason; and the very air became unnaturally chilled. While paddling by, the natives would be certain to avert their eyes, unwilling to look upon a place of such tragedy and evil. Those who were foolish enough to go ashore did so at their own peril, for they not only faced the wrath of angry ghosts but also risked a curse that would bring ill-luck, illness or even death upon them.

A great many mysterious events have occurred on or around the islands over the years, so there may be some truth to the tale. People have reported seeing apparitions on the islands and, just off shore, strange glowing lights in the water. Others note a malevolent sensation that they can't identify but that lingers until they've put the islands behind them. Pitiful sobs and cries of unimaginable pain break the stillness of the night. And legend says that a horribly twisted black tree—the very tree against which the young Iroquois man died—refuses to rot and decay despite the passage of centuries. If these legends are true, to touch this tree is to come in contact with the very soul-chilling essence of evil.

Some people even believe that a subterranean cave beneath the islands is home to Lake Nipissing's own sea monster, a horrific beast with piercing eyes in a black reptilian head. Imagine boating one day, enjoying the refreshing breeze and the warmth of the sun. Imagine spotting a black log floating on the surface and turning the wheel to avoid the obstacle. And now imagine that the water suddenly surges violently, the log rises out of the water, and a predatory snake-like head atop a long neck gazes down at you. Imagine how terrified you'd be. If reports dating back hundreds of years are accurate, several people have had a similar experience that left them scarred for life.

Although the Nipissing people made sure to avoid the Manitou Islands, Europeans put far less stock in superstition and legends. By the late 1800s, the area around Lake Nipissing was increasingly being settled and developed, and the Manitous were not exempt. There was a fur fort, limestone quarries to make mortar for railroad bridges, a resort and uranium mines. All enterprises were short-lived, however, and all left the owners ruined financially. It was as if the islands rejected human habitation. Perhaps there was something to the ancient Nipissing curse after all.

The Manitou Islands are mysterious and melancholy, especially with the cold waters of Lake Nipissing serving as a backdrop. There is a mysterious otherworldy quality about them that makes it easy to believe that they are inhabited by the forlorn spirits of cursed lovers, or even that they hide the lair of a frightful sea monster. The Manitou Islands are a link between the past and the present, the natural and the supernatural—and they're best left alone.

Woodchester Villa

A unique piece of architecture sits atop a steep winding drive, overlooking the town of Bracebridge. At one point in history this octagonal home had the most breathtaking view for miles and people in the community below gazed up at it with envy, but today the view is obscured and the building hidden by the aging trees that surround the grounds. Here, in this sheltered grove, the home-turned-museum is removed from the modern world, remaining forever a part of the 19th century it reflects and serving as a reminder of Bracebridge's early years.

Woodchester Villa is more than just an important heritage building and a tourist destination. Behind its beautifully restored walls lies a mystery that keeps visitors wondering what really happened in a home so grand and so unusual for its time. The house is long rumoured to be haunted, and many people find themselves questioning who the ghosts inhabiting Woodchester Villa are and what events led them to be there from beyond the grave. Is the home's unique, eight-sided design somehow tied into the story? Does this majestic building hold a deep secret? Any search for answers must begin at the beginning with the man who built the house: Henry J. Bird.

Henry Bird built Woodchester Villa in 1882, naming it after his birthplace, a fondly remembered village in England. In his early twenties, Bird, the son of a famous textiles miller, left England to travel to Australia, and then to the United States, but eventually he found a new home for himself in Canada. In 1867, Henry Bird began working as a supervisor of weavers for the Rosamond Woollen Company at Almonte,

The dead family of Henry Bird moved with him into Woodchester Villa and never left.

Ontario. No longer wandering and with a good job, things really started to turn around for Bird. He fell in love with and married Sarah Jane Fraser on December 25, 1868. From that moment on, the couple was happily inseparable. With his new life starting, the ambitious man soon decided to buy his own mill and was thrilled to find one for sale in Glen Allen, in Peel Township.

Unfortunately, his happiness was short lived. In the spring of 1870 and again in 1871, the mill was flooded out by the overwhelming rise of the river. As a result of the twin disasters, Bird's losses were growing and his dream of a productive mill to secure the future of his family began to weaken. Sadly, worse heartbreak was to follow. The next year, Sarah, the woman he envisioned sharing his life with, their three-year-old daughter, Elizabeth, and a six-month-old son all died within weeks of each other of tuberculosis. Bird was inconsolable. The losses left an open wound in his heart, and living in a now-silent home was torment beyond measure. Bird found it too painful to remain in Glen Allen.

Fleeing the scene of his heartbreak, in 1872 Bird relocated to Bracebridge and started over. He established new woollen mill, the first in Muskoka, alongside the waterfall in the heart of town. A year later, Bird found happiness again when he married Mary Matilda Ney. Soon after the wedding he began planning a home for his new family, one that reflected his status as one of Bracebridge's richest men. The unique, eight-sided house known as Woodchester Villa was the result.

Although Henry Bird remarried and had more children, not a day went by that he didn't think of his first family and grieve their loss. The unique design of his new home is a reflection of his lingering pain. He was preoccupied with never again enduring the agony of burying a loved one, and upon discovering that octagonal homes were supposed to be healthier for their residents, he quickly decided to go with such a design when building Woodchester Villa. Better air circulation, more natural lighting, easier to heat in winter, remaining cooler in summer—these were the claims made of octagonal homes. Whether or not there was any truth to the belief that octagonal homes led to healthier lives isn't really the point; Bird believed it, and his follow-through said much of the grief he silently bore. As it turned out, all seven children from his second marriage reached adulthood without serious illness.

Henry Bird carried the memory of Sarah and their two children in his heart forever. But in truth, they were never really far away. It seems they came with him to Bracebridge and moved into Woodchester Villa alongside Bird and his new wife and children. Local lore suggests that unusual things began to happen shortly after the family moved in: the sounds of a baby crying, the pitter-patter of small feet and a woman singing in the distance. We can't know for sure whether Bird did indeed experience these phenomena, but we do know they are reported within Woodchester Villa today. At any rate, the spectral sounds mustn't have been frequent or particularly startling, since the family remained happily in the home for almost a century. No one really paid attention or thought much about these unexplained activities; life just went on, and any strange noises simply became accepted quirks of a beloved family home.

From past to present, and we find that Woodchester Villa remains a Bracebridge landmark. Now a museum owned by the Town of Bracebridge, it is a portal into the lives of the Bird family and the development of the community of which they were a vital part. Woodchester Villa sees numerous visitors come and go every year. Most walk away from the guided tour with an appreciation of local history. But some visitors leave with memories of unusual experiences that remain vivid in their minds for years to come, memories that keep them wondering about the home's former inhabitants. Foremost on their minds: who remains behind and why?

It was a beautiful sunny spring day when Mandy and her friend Chris decided to visit this wonderful building on the hill. Woodchester Villa, though aged, was still magnificent in Mandy's eyes. Entering, she found a fully furnished home that looked as though the family had just stepped out. Business papers were scattered across the desk in the small den, fine china had been set out on the table in preparation for a meal, and toys were ready for play in the children's bed-rooms. It felt as though she and Chris were invading some-one's privacy and that the owners would soon return to find strangers in their home. She knew this feeling was silly, that the home was now just a monument to a time long past, but it persisted nonetheless.

Mandy slowly took in the beauty of this historic building, soaking in every amazing detail. At one point, as she walked along a narrow corridor, she turned to Chris with eyes wide and asked, "Did you hear that?"

"Hear what?" he replied, a little alarmed. Mandy thought she might have been hearing things, until once again she dis-tinctively discerned young children's laughter coming from what would have been the dumbwaiter. Again she asked Chris if he heard it, and again he replied no.

Mandy couldn't shake the feeling that children were around her, following her from room to room and happily playing. She would often hear their high-pitched laughter as she continued to tour the house. Every room she walked into the sound would follow, as if the little ones were playing a ghostly game of hide-and-seek. It was so real that once or twice she turned to see if in fact there was a family with kids exploring the house behind them, but of course there was no one there except Chris by her side and the tour guide ahead.

Now exploring the upstairs of the house, Mandy heard the faint sound of a woman singing. It seemed to be coming from a balcony overlooking the grounds, but once again there was no one to be seen. But even though her eyes told her she was alone, a sixth sense assured Mandy that a spectral woman was nearby and closely watching her. A tear moist-ened the young tourist's eye as she instinctively sensed that the ghost longed to live in this house but never had the opportunity. Tragedy had seen to that. The ghost wanted so badly to be the lady of this magnificent home, but though she floated unseen through its rooms it was not, and never had been, truly hers. Was this woman the mother of the children that Mandy sensed throughout the home? Were the playful youngsters looking for their mom? Or were they all looking for the comforting arms of the man of the house, a man absent for almost 100 years?

Mandy was confused until Chris asked if she felt that the woman and children were Henry Bird's first family. It was hard for her to say, but it was a possibility that might explain why the ghostly woman longed to be in this house; her early death of tuberculosis had robbed her of the opportunity to call this stately manor her home. Sarah Bird died in 1872, but her restless spirit refused to be apart from her husband. After all, they had vowed before God to be together forever. Mandy felt sad for the woman and her children, residing in an empty home, waiting patiently for their husband and father to return. She knew that they would never be reunited.

But of course Mandy isn't alone in sensing strange things in this historic building. Indeed, it wasn't long after the museum opened that staff discovered they shared the premises with more than one ghost. And since then, reports from volunteers, staff, tourists and paranormal investigators paint a picture of a building that is a hive of ghostly activity. Ted Currie, the founding director of Bracebridge Historical Society and a man who played a central role in the restoration of Woodchester Villa, had many experiences during the countless hours he spent on site, enough to fill a small book of his own.

"Having spent many, many hours alone in this house in the 1980s at all hours of day and night, there is no doubt in my mind the house was occupied spiritually. Yet it was never prevailed with any discernible negative aura," relates Currie in on online blog. He believes that the fact that Woodchester Villa is rumoured to be haunted by spirits from its past is actually quite appropriate in light of how important Henry Bird was to Bracebridge's history.

Currie goes on to share details of some of his experiences. "If I was raking leaves on the sprawling grounds in the autumn, I always felt as if someone was watching me from an upstairs window. If I was making lemonade for a summer social, I'd hear a baby crying when there was no one else in the house, and when I would be downstairs in the tiny staff kitchen I'd hear footsteps in the parlour above and on the staircase to the basement." Currie noted that the ghosts were never active at Christmas. It was the one time of year when they seemed peaceful and contented. Perhaps not coincidentally, Henry Bird and his first wife, Sarah, were married on Christmas Day in 1868.

"In my years of tenure I accepted them, even verbally addressing them when I sensed they were in an active state for whatever reason, and they as much accepted me as their protector for that period of our relationship. It was a haunt I learned to love and it was painful having to walk away," he remembers fondly.

Even after Ted Currie left his position with the historical society and no longer worked at the museum, its ghosts remained active and often revealed themselves to unsuspecting staff and guests. For example, in the autumn of 2009, a Bracebridge teenager, an amateur ghost-hunter who avidly watched every paranormal show on television, ventured up to Woodchester Villa one evening to conduct a solo investigation of its grounds. The sky overhead was cloudy, though the moon shone through enough to allow a splash of pale light to illuminate the terrain. A slight whisper of wind blowing through some nearby trees interrupted an otherwise eerie nighttime silence. The boy began taking photos of the building exterior and was excited to capture three orbs in several images. *This is just like a TV show*, he thought to himself, sure that he had just taken an important step in his career as a paranormal investigator. But he was soon shocked into forgetting about his camera and the pictures he was taking by a strange shadow that suddenly loomed in an upstairs window.

The shadow in the window was in the shape of a petite woman, and the would-be ghost-buster got the uneasy impression that the figure was watching him intensely. The boy was temporarily shaken because he knew there couldn't possibly be anyone inside. Woodchester Villa was closed for the season and locked up tight for the long winter ahead. It was also far too late at night for a member of the historical society to be inside, and besides, wouldn't they turn on the lights or at least use a flashlight? But soon his emotion turned from shock to excitement: he had physically come across his first apparition. Long seconds passed, with boy and shadow staring at each other, neither one moving. The boy's breath began to feel unfamiliar and heavy in his chest. Suddenly feeling all alone, his excitement changed to fear and he turned and ran down the steep drive, putting the mysterious home and its shadowy residents behind him.

A former staff member also had an unusual episode within Woodchester Villa. She agreed to share it with us but asked that her name not be revealed. We'll therefore call her Ellen. Ellen was dusting the china in the dining room when she heard an unusual scratching sound. She couldn't place the noise but there was something disturbing about it, so she put down her duster and went in search of it. The sound led her up the stairs, which she climbed slowly, not knowing what to expect when she reached the top floor. The closer she got to the top of the stairs, the more she was inexplicably overcome by a growing sense of unease. The strange sound, which reminded her of fingernails scratching a chalkboard, was coming from deep inside an antique metal wash tub sitting on the landing atop the stairs. This tub, Ellen had explained during many tours over the summer, had once belonged to the Bird family, and it was here that their tired bodies would soak their work pains away. The scratching seemed panicked, like a small animal trying desperately to crawl up the smooth sides.

Ellen approached the tub cautiously, scared of what she might find and having no idea what she would do if indeed a rodent had become trapped inside. When she got close enough, she cautiously peered over the edge. To her surprise, it was empty. Stranger still, the scratching suddenly stopped. She looked around every angle of the tub and again found nothing that could have caused the sound.

Shrugging her shoulders in confusion, Ellen went back downstairs to finish dusting the dining room. No sooner had she got to the final step than the scratching started up again. Intrigued, she made her way back to the tub, less timid this time. Once again the noise ceased as soon as she drew near, and once again she found the tub empty. This routine continued two or three more times, until finally she grew tired of it and simply began to ignore the sound.

Eventually the scratching ceased entirely, but not without leaving questions in Ellen's mind. Could this have been the sound of a loving mother trying to get a bath ready for her kids? Had the spirit children been playing a prank?

There are countless similar accounts from people visiting or working at Woodchester Villa. Cold spots are frequently felt on the stairs leading to the basement. One time, it was so cold a woman could see her breath and claimed crystals formed on the wood panelling. Understandably scared, she fled into the warm summer sunlight. Another woman entered the kitchen to find it as it must have looked prior to renovation: the floorboards were warped with moisture and the panelling was scratched and splotchy with mould. When her husband spoke to her, his voice shattered the illusion and snapped her back to reality. Instantly, the ruined room was replaced by one lovingly restored and meticulously maintained.

With a home as grand and beautiful as Woodchester Villa, we don't expect to find a mysterious side. But consider this: the very same reasons we find this home so appealing would also make it difficult for ghosts to leave, especially a mother and her children who, through tragic circumstances, were deprived of the opportunity to live here in life. This home represents what could have been had years not been stolen from them by tuberculosis and is a tangible link to the husband and father from whom death separated them. These spirits may never leave. Why would they?

Logging Camp Ghost

In today's society, with forensic science and modern crime-solving techniques, justice for murder victims is generally achieved, even if it might sometimes be slow in coming. But before DNA evidence and fingerprinting, many killers walked free for lack of incriminating evidence. It's hard to imagine these criminals, plagued by their guilty conscience, sleeping soundly at night. Similarly, in the absence of justice, it's hard to imagine the victims resting peacefully in their graves. In eternal turmoil, many claw their way out of the ground and haunt the scenes of their tragic and untimely deaths, awaiting the day when their murderer is convicted and they can be at ease.

One such unresolved murder that resulted in a restless victim occurred in the wild fringes of Muskoka in the late 19th century. The events of that cold, wintery day in 1882, when a grizzly discovery was made at one of the Gilmour Lumber Company's shanty camps, left hardened lumbermen gaping in horror and captured the imagination of newspaper readers across the region.

At that time, logging camps were popping up all over Northern Ontario as lumber companies competed against one another to harvest the riches of the untouched forests. The demand for lumber was insatiable, and even an average operation would cut thousands of logs over the course of a winter. As a result, there was always employment to be found at the bush camps, and farmers from across the area would flock to them in search of income to supplement the meager gains from their homesteads. In amongst these honest workers, the shady and lawless could blend in effortlessly, and

The ghost of a boy terrorized the logging camp where he was brutally murdered.

no one would ever suspect their wicked past. Logging camps, located in the remoteness of the wilderness, became the hiding place for countless criminals.

Conditions in the camps led to frayed nerves and altercations. The accommodations for workers were hardly luxurious; a typical bunkhouse would be a make-shift log shanty filled with bunk beds stacked high to the ceiling, and oftentimes there would be more bodies than the shanty could comfortably hold. Food was boring and poor, rules were restrictive and harshly enforced, and there was little in the way of leisure to distract the men from their hardships. Even without the unwelcome presence of thugs and criminals, it was no wonder that some of the men would get restless and irritable on occasion. When tempers flared, the matter would typically be solved with a no-holds-barred fistfight. When the dust settled and one man emerged victorious, the matter was closed. That was the end of it. But there were times, particularly when a low-life was involved, when things would get out of hand. A boy whose name has been forgotten, but who we'll call Tim, discovered this harsh truth firsthand.

Tim was a youngster, not yet even shaving, yet he was all alone in the world. After losing his family to one of the illnesses that occasionally swept through Muskoka like an unchecked forest fire, Tim found himself at loose ends. He needed to find work so he could at least put food in his mouth, so he headed off into the dark, dense forest in search of the Gilmour Lumber Company's shanty camp.

Tim fought back tears as his thoughts turned to his family, but fear soon replaced the sadness as he began to hear the sounds of the night—wolves howled and owls hooted, and something crunched in the snow as it raced away in the darkness. With each step he took, Tim grew more and more afraid. He was almost ready to give up, but then he heard his father's voice, drowning out all the strange and terrifying sounds: "Now Timmy, you're a young man and you have to be strong to survive in a man's world." Tim found strength in his father's words. He knew he had to be brave. More determined than ever, he began to pick up his pace and struggled through the snowdrifts toward the camp.

Morning's light was just creeping through the trees when he happened upon the awakening Gilmour camp. Tim couldn't believe his eyes. The men were monsters, huge unshaven beasts that looked like they could knock the trees down with their bare hands. He felt nearly invisible beside them. Most of these men looked liked they hadn't seen water in months, but one man in clean clothes stood out. The foreman, Tim thought as he approached the man. He explained how he had lost his family and that his father had worked for the Gilmour Company in the past, and asked whether the foreman could be so kind as to help him in his time of need. The foreman sized up the scrawny 15-year-old lad and told him he was too young to do a man's job, but perhaps the cook could use some help in the kitchen.

No one in camp, including the foreman, knew much about the cook. He had just appeared out of nowhere one day looking for work. An ill-tempered man, he couldn't get along with the other workers so the foreman decided to make him the camp cook; that way he could spend the days in isolation in the kitchen. There were whispers about a dark past, but no one knew for sure. When the camp foreman brought Tim before him, the cook was displeased. He was not used to working with others and surely did not want a kid underfoot to make his life more difficult. The cook simply looked at Tim and turned away in disgust, muttering under his breath as he stormed off.

Tim was instantly frightened of the man. A pug-faced, mash-nosed giant, he had a bone to pick with everyone and everything and seemed to be operating with a permanently short fuse. There was an air of violence that hovered over him like a dark cloud, and whenever the cook entered a room it seemed to darken into hushed tones and wary looks. No one spoke to him, and few men were willing even to make eye contact.

Despite the foreman's assurance that the cook would grow to accept Tim, the cook's demeanor only grew worse as the days passed. He refused Tim's help and rarely acknowledged his presence except to yell at him. Tim couldn't understand what he had done for this man to hate him so. All he wanted to do was to help and earn his keep. No matter what the boy did, it was always wrong—the food was too salty, too runny, too dry. Sometimes, when he had inadvertently riled the man's anger, Tim could see a homicidal glint in his deep-set eyes. He found himself quivering with fear just being in the cook's presence.

One night, the exhausted lumberjacks returned to camp to hear angry screams and pitiful yelps of pain coming from within the cookhouse. They ran inside to find the rage-filled cook beating the young boy mercilessly and quickly pulled the boy to safety. Embarrassed at having had to be rescued when he was trying so hard to be a man, Tim raced away in tears. The cook, meanwhile, went to bed muttering threats of revenge. No one put much stock in the cook's ranting. He was always threatening someone or another with harm, and nothing ever came of it. Everyone was sure that come morning, cooler heads would prevail.

The next morning, all was eerily quiet in the camp. The lumbermen roused themselves from their bunks well before the sun had even begun to creep above the horizon and hungrily converged on the cookhouse for a hearty breakfast of flapjacks and biscuits. They weren't pleased when they found no food awaiting them and the building weirdly dark. Angrily, they ventured into the kitchen in search of their meal. The room was empty, and it was clear no one had been there that morning; no food had been laid out for preparation, the coffee pot was empty and the kitchen stove remained cold and unlit.

By now concerned, the men searched the camp for the cook and his assistant but found neither of them. Soon the search was called off. Everyone assumed that Tim had been so afraid of the cook that he had run away. They were also convinced that the cook, still enraged, had packed up and left as well. It was a strange coincidence, but no one thought too much of it. Men came and went all the time. Their immediate concern was to scrounge up a breakfast to fuel them for the coming day's labour. Another man was assigned to take care of the cooking duties, and life went on.

Things had begun to settle into a new and comfortable routine when, a few days later, the new cook went to a barrel to get some pork. He pried the lid off and, reaching in, pulled out a small hand between two pieces of meat. The other men heard his screams of horror and raced to his side. Many of them gagged in reflex at the grisly sight. But worse was to come. When they began to dig deeper into the barrel, more pieces of flesh were discovered, and then a head. It was Tim, his face still frozen in the terror of his dying moments.

At first the men wondered who could have done such a brutal thing, but then it became all too clear: the cook had murdered Tim and then stuffed his corpse into the barrel so that the shantymen would not notice his crime until he was far away. The plan was brutally effective, because though the lumbermen looked in the thick woods for any sign of the cook, nothing was ever found.

The story gripped readers of local papers (the *Orillia Times* ran a particularly gruesome version in its February 2, 1882, edition) and fuelled gossip for weeks. But eventually interests turned to other, more current matters. Lawmen were no longer on the lookout for the degenerate cook, and Tim, with no family to keep his memory alive, was soon forgotten. A boy would never become a man, the murderer was never apprehended and justice was never served.

But in truth, the story was just beginning. Not long after Tim's remains were pulled from the pork barrel, strange things began being reported at the lumber camp. Men would wake in the middle of the night to spine-chilling screams that sounded as if they came from just outside the bunkhouse. The first few times they heard the screaming they would fumble in the dark for a lantern, hurriedly light it and then race outside to find the source of the terrifying sound. They would look all around the bunkhouse, extending the search to the rest of the camp and even the woods nearby, but never found any tracks in the snow or saw anything unusual. After a few nights of fruitless searching, the lumberjacks began to accept that the screams came from beyond the grave and that they were being haunted for their failure to save the cook's young assistant. Thereafter, when they heard the midnight cries they would remain shivering in their beds, tightly closing their eyes and willing morning to arrive quickly.

It wasn't long before Tim was seen watching loggers from the depths of the forest while they worked, or even in the darkened interior of the bunkhouse as they slept. Such glimpses of the deceased were always fleeting—there one minute, gone the next. Although the spirit never did anything threatening, even momentary glimpses of his forlorn face and pain-filled eyes left the men trembling in fear. Within the cookhouse, poltergeist activity was reported. Pots would fly across the kitchen, the fire in the woodstove would die suddenly and inexplicably and items would go missing.

The spring melt, when the logs would be driven downstream to waiting sawmills and the men paid off to return to their homes, couldn't come fast enough. When at last winter faded and they were allowed to leave, each man vowed he would never return to the camp, no matter how dire his financial situation.

Over the course of the year, these men confided their experiences to friends and neighbours, and word spread rapidly that the camp was cursed. As a result, when late fall arrived and the Gilmour Lumber Company was looking for men to work in the camp, they found few takers. Most men who did show up had not heard of the ghost that plagued the camp, and those who had were so desperate they were willing to brave the supernatural. It wasn't long before they regretted their decision, and come spring they too vowed never to return to the place. With each passing winter fewer and fewer men showed up in search of work, forcing the Gilmour Lumber Company to accept the inevitable and close the camp for good.

After years of facing a relentless assault by lumbermen wielding saws and axes, the forests around the camp were silent once more. But still, the dark taint of that horrific murder in the winter of 1882 remained, as if the boy's blood had soaked through the deep snow to forever stain the very earth beneath. The festering torment of the ghost had warped the landscape. It's said that the trees in the area, once beautiful, green and proudly upright, have become dark, twisted and stooped. Even on the clearest summer day the sun seems to scorn this place. No birds sing amongst the leaf canopy, and animals are suspiciously absent. It's an unnatural place where nothing seems quite right.

Perhaps understandably, people wanted to forget about the frightfully haunted logging camp, to wipe the horrors it contained completely from their collective mind. They buried the memories so deep that today few people have heard the story. Fewer still know exactly where this particular Gilmour Lumber Company camp was located: "somewheres east of

Dorset," is about as accurate as you'll get. With more than 125 years having gone by, it's likely that little tangible evidence of the camp remains. The log buildings will have rotted and collapsed in on themselves, and where forests were ravaged will now be cloaked in younger trees that hide the obvious scars of the logging era.

But if you happen to be in the area, deep in the woods, and come across a place where twisted black trees rise wretchedly from the soil, where shadows play cruel tricks and there are no sounds except for mournful cries riding on an unnatural wind, you may have stumbled upon a long-abandoned logging camp and the site of a gruesome murder. Does the innocent victim, killed well before his time and hacked apart like a side of venison, still linger here as a mournful and increasingly bitter ghost? Has time healed his wounds, or will he resist being laid to rest until such time as his murderer is brought to justice? Does he still look out at the world that treated him so cruelly with eyes that silently cry out in sadness?

Pray you never stumble upon this evil place to find out. Like the lumberjacks who worked here years ago discovered, those who come here don't always leave the same way. Sometimes, they take with them the emotional scars of experiencing unnatural terror.

The End

Acknowledgements

Our thanks go out to a great many people for their kind assistance in the preparation of this book. Without their assistance, *Cottage Country Ghosts* would not have been possible. These individuals include Ted Nelson and the staff at Inn at the Falls for offering their experiences and for their warm hospitality; Teri Souter and Sara White of Muskoka Heritage Place; Ken Veitch, a Bracebridge historian whose insight was always invaluable; the staff of Muskoka Steamships and the crew of the *Segwun*, most especially Kate Cox for trusting us enough to open up about her experiences; the owners and staff of Yesterday's Resort, who willingly offered their stories; Frank Cooper, who shared memories of his family and liked to remind us that "Cooper's Falls is not a ghost town because I'm still here"; Sue St. Clair of the Toronto Ghosts and Haunting Research Society, who was always willing to suggest stories worth pursuing; Dan Larocque for a guided tour of Cobalt's rich past and rubbing his passion for the community off on us; Paul Ivanoff and Lena Kolobow of the Chancery Art Gallery; the reference librarians at the Bracebridge Public Library for helping us track down obscure historical facts; Woodchester Villa's staff, past and present; and Giles Alldin, who put aside a natural skepticism to share his encounters with the supernatural.

Perhaps most importantly, we'd like to thank all those people who took the brave step of contacting us and recounting their brushes with the paranormal, some of whom were understandably reluctant to have their names appear in print. Their experiences provide the stories appearing in this book with an intimacy and richness that could not otherwise have been created; if *Cottage Country Ghosts* causes a chill to run down your spine, it's because of them and the stories they shared.

Finally, we'd like to thank Nancy Foulds of Ghost House Books for allowing us to write *Cottage Country Ghosts*. It had been a dream of ours since reading our first Ghost House book, the intensely powerful *Romantic Ghost Stories* by Julie Burtinshaw, to contribute to the series and now, thanks to Nancy's trust, we can proudly say dreams can come true.

Personal Acknowledgements

Maria Da Silva writes: researching a book always brings me so much pleasure. The people we meet, the places we see, the secrets we uncover—it's a thrilling new experience every time. But this book was a particular thrill to write because Cottage Country is a place I've grown to love. Through the years our Muskoka friends have brought so much joy to my life, as they shared their interest in the supernatural as well as the rich history that fills the region. This book goes out to all of you who make it what is.

My fascination for the unexplained just keeps growing, and I thank Andrew for allowing me to explore it more and more with each new book we write together. And as always, I want to thank my family for being so supportive and for believing in me.

Andrew Hind writes: my love for Cottage Country was born of summers spent at the family cottage on Virtue Lake, where most of my most treasured childhood memories were made. I'm not sure I've ever thanked my parents for making the sacrifices that allowed me to have those experiences and, in a roundabout way, inspiring this book.

As always, I'd like to express gratitude to my co-author and the truest friend a person could have, Maria Da Silva. I enjoyed every minute of exploring the darker side of Cottage Country at her side, and now have new treasured memories to go along with those made as a child. Her passion for ghosts made this book a reality and made researching and writing it a joy. On a more personal level, she saw things in me I never did and pushed me to achieve goals I never dreamt possible. For that I thank her.

About the Authors

Maria Da Silva and Andrew Hind are freelance writers who specialize in the paranormal, history and travel. They have a passion for bringing to light unusual stories, little-remembered episodes in history and fascinating locations few people know about. Together, they have contributed numerous articles to magazine publications, including many in Cottage Country such as *Muskoka Magazine*, *Parry Sound Sideroads*, *The Muskokan* and *The Muskoka Sun*. They also conduct guided historical and ghost tours, helping people connect with the past in a personal way.

Maria has always had a passion for ghosts and the paranormal. Her interest in the subject and her love of Northern Ontario inspired *Cottage Country Ghosts*. Andrew developed a love of history early on, and he hopes, through his writing, to develop a similar passion in others. *Cottage Country Ghosts* is Maria and Andrew's seventh book.